Table of Contents

Success Strategies

This section contains a list of test-taking strategies that you may find helpful as you work through the test. By taking what you know and applying logical thought, you can maximize your chances of answering any question correctly!

It is very important to realize that every question is different and every person is different: no single strategy will work on every question, and no single strategy will work for every person. That's why we've included all of them here, so you can try them out and determine which ones work best for different types of questions and which ones work best for you.

Question Strategies

Read Carefully

Read the question and answer choices carefully. Don't miss the question because you misread the terms. You have plenty of time to read each question thoroughly and make sure you understand what is being asked. Yet a happy medium must be attained, so don't waste too much time. You must read carefully, but efficiently.

Contextual Clues

Look for contextual clues. If the question includes a word you are not familiar with, look at the immediate context for some indication of what the word might mean. Contextual clues can often give you all the information you need to decipher the meaning of an unfamiliar word. Even if you can't determine the meaning, you may be able to narrow down the possibilities enough to make a solid guess at the answer to the question.

Prefixes

If you're having trouble with a word in the question or answer choices, try dissecting it. Take advantage of every clue that the word might include. Prefixes and suffixes can be a huge help. Usually they allow you to determine a basic meaning. Pre- means before, post- means after, pro - is positive, ce- is negative. From prefixes and suffixes, you can get an idea of the general meaning of the word and try to put it into context.

Hedge Words

Watch out for critical hedge words, such as *likely, may, can, often, almost, mostly, usually, generally, rarely*, and *sometimes*. Question writers insert these hedge phrases to cover every possibility. Often an answer choice will be wrong simply because it leaves no room for exception. Be on guard for answer choices that have definitive words such as *exactly* and *always*.

Switchback Words

Stay alert for *switchbacks*. These are the words and phrases frequently used to alert you to shifts in thought. The most common switchback words are *but, although*, and *however*. Others include *nevertheless, on the other hand, even though, while, in spite of, despite, regardless of*. Switchback words are important to catch because they can change the direction of the question or an answer choice.

Face Value

When in doubt, use common sense. Accept the situation in the problem at face value. Don't read too much into it. These problems will not require you to make wild assumptions. If you have to go beyond creativity and warp time or space in order to have an answer choice fit the question, then you should move on and consider the other answer choices. These are normal problems rooted in reality. The applicable relationship or explanation may not be readily apparent, but it is there for you to figure out. Use your common sense to interpret anything that isn't clear.

Answer Choice Strategies

Answer Selection

The most thorough way to pick an answer choice is to identify and eliminate wrong answers until only one is left, then confirm it is the correct answer. Sometimes an answer choice may immediately seem right, but be careful. The test writers will usually put more than one reasonable answer choice on each question, so take a second to read all of them and make sure that the other choices are not equally obvious. As long as you have time left, it is better to read every answer choice than to pick the first one that looks right without checking the others.

Answer Choice Families

An answer choice family consists of two (in rare cases, three) answer choices that are very similar in construction and cannot all be true at the same time. If you see two answer choices that are direct opposites or parallels, one of them is usually the correct answer. For instance, if one answer choice says that quantity *x* increases and another either says that quantity *x* decreases (opposite) or says that quantity *y* increases (parallel), then those answer choices would fall into the same family. An answer choice that doesn't match the construction of the answer choice family is more likely to be incorrect. Most questions will not have answer choice families, but when they do appear, you should be prepared to recognize them.

Eliminate Answers

Eliminate answer choices as soon as you realize they are wrong, but make sure you consider all possibilities. If you are eliminating answer choices and realize that the last one you are left with is also wrong, don't panic. Start over and consider each choice again. There may be something you missed the first time that you will realize on the second pass.

Avoid Fact Traps

Don't be distracted by an answer choice that is factually true but doesn't answer the question. You are looking for the choice that answers the question. Stay focused on what the question is asking for so you don't accidentally pick an answer that is true but incorrect. Always go back to the question and make sure the answer choice you've selected actually answers the question and is not merely a true statement.

Extreme Statements

In general, you should avoid answers that put forth extreme actions as standard practice or proclaim controversial ideas as established fact. An answer choice that states the "process should be used in certain situations, if..." is much more likely to be correct than one that states the "process should be discontinued completely." The first is a calm rational statement and doesn't even make a definitive, uncompromising stance, using a hedge word *if* to provide wiggle room, whereas the second choice is a radical idea and far more extreme.

Benchmark

As you read through the answer choices and you come across one that seems to answer the question well, mentally select that answer choice. This is not your final answer, but it's the one that will help you evaluate the other answer choices. The one that you selected is your benchmark or standard for judging each of the other answer choices. Every other answer choice must be compared to your benchmark. That choice is correct until proven otherwise by another answer choice beating it. If you find a better answer, then that one becomes your new benchmark. Once you've decided that no other choice answers the question as well as your benchmark, you have your final answer.

Predict the Answer

Before you even start looking at the answer choices, it is often best to try to predict the answer. When you come up with the answer on your own, it is easier to avoid distractions and traps because you will know exactly what to look for. The right answer choice is unlikely to be word-for-word what you came up with, but it should be a close match. Even if you are confident that you have the right answer, you should still take the time to read each option before moving on.

General Strategies

Tough Questions

If you are stumped on a problem or it appears too hard or too difficult, don't waste time. Move on! Remember though, if you can quickly check for obviously incorrect answer choices, your chances of guessing correctly are greatly improved. Before you completely give up, at least try to knock out a couple of possible answers. Eliminate what you can and then guess at the remaining answer choices before moving on.

Check Your Work

Since you will probably not know every term listed and the answer to every question, it is important that you get credit for the ones that you do know.

Don't miss any questions through careless mistakes. If at all possible, try to take a second to look back over your answer selection and make sure you've selected the correct answer choice and haven't made a costly careless mistake (such as marking an answer choice that you didn't mean to mark). This quick double check should more than pay for itself in caught mistakes for the time it costs.

Pace Yourself

It's easy to be overwhelmed when you're looking at a page full of questions; your mind is confused and full of random thoughts, and the clock is ticking down faster than you would like. Calm down and maintain the pace that you have set for yourself. Especially as you get down to the last few minutes of the test, don't let the small numbers on the clock make you panic. As long as you are on track by monitoring your pace, you are guaranteed to have time for each question.

Don't Rush

It is very easy to make errors when you are in a hurry. Maintaining a fast pace in answering questions is pointless if it makes you miss questions that you would have gotten right otherwise. Test writers like to include distracting information and wrong answers that seem right. Taking a little extra time to avoid careless mistakes can make all the difference in your test score. Find a pace that allows you to be confident in the answers that you select.

Keep Moving

Panicking will not help you pass the test, so do your best to stay calm and keep moving. Taking deep breaths and going through the answer elimination steps you practiced can help to break through a stress barrier and keep your pace.

Final Notes

The combination of a solid foundation of content knowledge and the confidence that comes from practicing your plan for applying that knowledge is the key to maximizing your performance on test day. As your foundation of content knowledge is built up and strengthened, you'll find that the strategies included in this chapter become more and more effective in helping you quickly sift through the distractions and traps of the test to isolate the correct answer.

Now it's time to move on to the test content chapters of this book, but be sure to keep your goal in mind. As you read, think about how you will be able to apply this information on the test. If you've already seen sample questions for the test and you have an idea of the question format and style, try to come up with questions of your own that you can answer based on what you're reading. This will give you valuable practice applying your knowledge in the same ways you can expect to on test day.

Good luck and good studying!

The Alligator and the Squirrel
(An adaptation of Aesop's Fable, The Lion and the Mouse)

1 Once, in a lush African forest, there lived an old alligator. Being a very old alligator indeed, he kept to himself, spending his days swimming, sleeping, and sunning himself. Most of the other forest animals were wise enough to leave the old reptile alone, but one day, an astonishing thing happened.

2 Alligator was just dozing off one morning after a lazy swim, when he felt movement on his tail.

3 "Say, who is that running along my tail?"

4 It was Squirrel. At the sound of Alligator's big, booming voice, Squirrel froze in his tracks. "Oh no," thought Squirrel, "now what will I do?" Truthfully, Squirrel had made quite a habit of running up and down Alligator's tail. The bumps on Alligator's tail were quite large to a small animal like Squirrel, and running over them helped keep him in tip-top shape. Thus, Squirrel could beat all the other squirrels to the tastiest nuts! Normally, Squirrel made sure that Alligator was completely asleep before beginning his workout ritual, but today he'd been impatient. Now, he was in trouble. Just then, Alligator, with one powerful swish of his mighty tail, tossed Squirrel into the air, placing him on Alligator's chin.

5 "Well," said Alligator, "it's little Squirrel. How are you today, my silly little friend?"

6 Squirrel looked into Alligator’s big, bulging eyes. He had to think fast, so he mustered up all the courage he had, smiled his friendliest smile, and said,

7 “Why, good morning, dear Alligator! Isn’t it a lovely morning?”

8 Alligator chuckled to himself. What luck! Since he had begun his day with a swim, he’d neglected to come up with any breakfast for himself. And now, it seemed his breakfast had come to him.

9 “Oh, yes, dear Squirrel,” said Alligator, “it is a beautiful morning. And how wonderful for you, since it will be the last morning you will ever see.”

10 Squirrel swallowed hard. “The last morning I will ever see? Whatever do you mean, Alligator

11 Alligator smiled. “Well, it just so happens, Squirrel, that I have not yet had my breakfast this morning. And since you were so foolish as to run along my tail, I cannot help but think that you will be as good a breakfast as any.” And, with that, Alligator opened his huge mouth and started to swallow the little animal. Squirrel grabbed one of Alligator’s sharp teeth and held on for dear life.

12 “Wait, I beg you to let me live! I may be able to help you someday in the near future.” said Squirrel.

13 At this, Alligator laughed out loud. “You, tiny Squirrel, help me? I think not. But, you do amuse me, Squirrel, so I will let you live. Go, be on your way, and do not let me catch you running on my tail again.”

14 Just a few days later, Alligator fell into a trap set by some hunters. He was caught in a large net, and no matter how hard he swished his tail, he could not seem to break free.

15 “Alas, my life is over!” said Alligator.

16 About that time, Squirrel happened by and saw poor Alligator caught in the trap. He immediately ran over and began gnawing the ropes of the net. After a while, Squirrel had gnawed a big enough hole in the net for Alligator to escape.

17 "Thank you, dear Squirrel! It seems that you were right. You and I will be forever friends," said Alligator.

18 "Little friends may prove great friends," said Squirrel.

Questions

1. What word means almost the same thing as *astonishing* in paragraph 1?
    a. boring
    b. similar
    c. astounding
    d. predictable

2. What was astonishing about the squirrel running along the alligator's tail?

____

3. This story is told in:
    a. the first person
    b. the second person
    c. the third person
    d. the fourth person

4. This story is a **fable**. What is a fable?
    a. a story based on something that actually happened
    b. a poem that doesn't rhyme
    c. part one of a three part series
    d. a short fantasy story that teaches a moral lesson

5. Why didn't the alligator eat the squirrel?

____

6. In paragraph 8, what does *neglected* to mean?

a. hurried to
b. forgotten to
c. meant to
d. tried to

7. Divide *neglected* into syllables.

____

8. This is an adaptation of another story. What does *adapt* mean?

a. change in one or more ways
b. write in cursive
c. add quotation marks
d. invent

9. Which word would be a good substitute for *mustered* in paragraph 6?

a. discarded
b. gathered
c. discouraged
d. hid

10. Which of the following is NOT a lesson we can learn from this fable?

a. you can't trust anyone
b. being kind to others often leads to good things
c. we should repay those who have done us a favor
d. friends come in all shapes and sizes

Audrey's Braces

1 "OK, Audrey, what color bands would you like?" asked Dr. Dyson.

2 Twelve-year-old Audrey looked gloomily at her mom, then Dr. Dyson. Finally, she just looked down and shrugged. Who cares what color bands she gets on her braces? Her braces: how awful.

3 "How about blue and red, the Trojan colors? They'll match your cheerleading uniform," said Mom.

4 "Sure, blue and red, whatever...that's fine," said Audrey, not even trying to smile.

5 "Blue and red it is, then," said Dr. Dyson. "So, you're a cheerleader? That's great. I've had many patients who were cheerleaders."

6 "Really?" asked Audrey. Funny, none of the cheerleaders Audrey knew had braces. Actually, no one Audrey knew had braces.

7 Attaching the bands took only a few minutes. "Well, we're all done," said Dr. Dyson, cheerfully. "Now, your teeth may be a little sore for a few days, so just take a pain reliever if you need to, Audrey. If she has any problems at all, Mrs. Caraway, just give us a call. If not, we'll see you both next month."

8 "Thank you, Dr. Dyson," said Mom. "Ready?"

9 "I guess so," said Audrey. "Do I have to go back to school? There's only about an hour left and my teeth really are kind of sore."

10 Mom said, "Well, I guess not. Do you want to look in the mirror before we go?"

11 "No, it's fine. I can look at home," said Audrey.

12 Mom frowned. "OK, but you really look cute."

13 "Cute? I doubt it," thought Audrey.

14 As soon as she got home, Audrey went straight to her room and stood in front of her mirror with her eyes closed. Well, here goes, she thought. She opened her eyes, smiled, and there they were, her awful, horrible braces. The little metal brackets were actually bigger than she'd thought they would be, and the blue and red bands stood out. She felt like a freak. She just knew everyone would be laughing at her at school tomorrow, and that she would be a pariah.

15 Audrey plopped down across her bed. How would she ever go back to school with those ugly things on her teeth?

16 "Knock, knock," said Daddy. Audrey opened her eyes and saw Daddy standing in the doorway.

17 "Hi, Daddy," said Audrey.

18 "Well, I heard someone around here got braces today. Any idea who?" asked Daddy.

19 "I'm afraid it's me."

20 "Well, let's see them. Give me a big smile."

21 But instead of a smile, Audrey began to cry.

22 "What's wrong, baby?" asked Daddy.

23"I hate my braces, Daddy! They're ugly and everyone is going to make fun of me tomorrow at school," said Audrey.

24 Daddy put his arms around her. "No, they're not. Audrey, your friends love you for who you are inside. Besides, I'll bet you before the school year is over many of your friends will be getting braces. Most people have to get braces; it's a normal part of growing up."

25 The next morning, Audrey was still nervous about school, and her braces still hurt.

26 "Ready?" asked Mom.

27 "I guess. I have to go back to school eventually, so I might as well get it over with," said Audrey.

28 When Audrey got to school, several of her friends were sitting together in the cafeteria.

29 "Hey, Audrey," said Jill. "Where were you yesterday?"

30 Audrey took a deep breath and said, "I had an orthodontist appointment. I got braces."

31 All of her friends' faces lit up. "Wow!" said Claire. "I love the blue and red bands. I'm getting braces next month. I'm going to get Trojan colored bands, too."

32 "Yeah, I get mine next week," said Samantha. "Do they hurt, Audrey?"

33 Audrey smiled. She felt so much better. "No, they're not bad at all."

Questions

1. Why does Audrey think *how awful* about her braces?

___

2. How many syllables does *orthodontist* have?

___

3. Which word would be a good substitute for *pariah* in paragraph 14?
   a. shark
   b. hall monitor
   c. outcast
   d. ghost

4. What is the nickname of the athletic teams at Audrey's school?

___

5. Who is speaking in paragraph 19?

___

6. Who is speaking in paragraph 20?

___

7. Which word would be a good substitute for *gloomily* in paragraph 2?
   a. cheerily
   b. brightly
   c. normally
   d. forlornly

8. Even though her braces still hurt, Audrey told her friends they didn't. Why do you think she did that?

___

___

9. Divide *eventually* into syllables.

____

10. What is the main theme of this story?
    a. often things aren't nearly as bad as they seem at first
    b. it's important to go out for the cheerleading team
    c. Dad is always right
    d. getting braces is extremely painful

The Great Cupcake Heist

1 "Mom, we're finished making the cupcakes," said Jaci. She and her 10-year-old twin brother, Jack, had been making cupcakes all afternoon for their school harvest festival.

2 "Look at them, Mom," said Jack. "I think they are going to be the best dessert at the festival."

3 "Yes," said Jaci. "Everyone at the Cake Walk booth is going to want to win these pumpkin cupcakes."

4 "They look downright scrumptious!" said Mom. "Put them in the cupcake holder on the table and close the lid tight. Now, you two need to go clean up and put on your costumes. We need to leave in about an hour."

5 The twins quickly ran to their rooms to put the final touches on their costumes. They had been waiting for what seemed like forever for the harvest festival, and the big night had finally arrived. Jack was going as a pirate and Jaci was going as a nurse. They could hardly wait to get there.

6 A few minutes later, Jack and Jaci appeared in the living room, fully bedecked for the festival.

7 "Mom, we're ready!" called Jack.

8 "I'll get the cupcakes," said Jaci.

9 "Jaci, let's make a deal. If I win the cupcakes, I'll give you one, and if you win them, you can give me one, OK?" asked Jack.

10 "Very funny, you thief!"

11 "What are you talking about?"

12 "Well, it looks to me like you've already helped yourself to one," said Jaci.

13 "Huh?" asked Jack. He walked over to the table and saw that the cupcake holder was open and one of their perfect pumpkin pastries was gone. For a second he was too stunned to speak. Then he found his voice again.

14 "Hey!" Jack blurted out, "*I* didn't eat it. I went to change into my costume. I bet *you* snuck back into the kitchen and ate it."

15 "I did not!" said Jaci.

16 The twins glared at each other for a moment, then Jack said,

17 "Well, if *you* didn't eat the cupcake, and *I* didn't eat the cupcake, who did?"

18 Just then Mom walked in.

19 "Are you guys ready to load up?"

20 Jaci put her hand on her hip. "Mom, did you eat one of our cupcakes?"

21 "Me? Of course not," said Mom.

22 "Well, one of them is most assuredly gone," said Jack. "Who could have eaten it?"

23 "Hmmm...it sounds like you kids have a real whodunit on your hands," Mom said, with a wicked grin.

24 "We certainly do," said Jaci. "We'll simply have to use our powers of deduction to solve it. Who most likely would've eaten our cupcake?"

25 "I know!" said Jack. "I bet it was Bo. He was hanging around all afternoon hoping for a bite of one."

26 "Yeah," said Jaci, "and if he did eat one, the wrapper will be left over. Let's go check."

27 The twins raced off to find Bo, their pet dog, who was dozing on his bed. They looked all around, but found no trace of the cupcake or the wrapper. They even checked around Bo's mouth for icing, but there wasn't any.

28 "Well, it doesn't look like Bo did it," said Jack.

29 "What about Jeff?" asked Jaci.

30 Jeff, the twins' seventeen-year-old brother, was in his room studying. Jack and Jaci ran to his room.

31 "Wow, don't you two look cool," said Jeff.

32 "Never mind that," said Jack, crossing his arms over his chest. "Tell us the truth, Jeff. Did you eat one of our cupcakes?"

33 "What if I did? What are you going to do - make me walk the plank? Or take my temperature?" Jeff laughed.

34 Jaci wasn't amused. "That's not funny, Jeff! Now admit it!"

35 "Scout's honor, I didn't even know you had any cupcakes," said Jeff. "Come on, guys, use your heads--if I had known about them, I would've eaten a lot more than one!"

36 The twins couldn't argue with that logic. If Jeff had been the culprit, there doubtless would've been several cupcakes missing. They walked back to the kitchen. "OK," said Jaci. "If Mom didn't eat the cupcake, and Bo didn't eat the cupcake, and Jeff didn't eat the cupcake, who did?"

37 Just then, Daddy walked into the kitchen.

38 "DADDY!" the twins exclaimed. There was Daddy, with cupcake crumbs on his shirt and icing on his upper lip.

39 "What?" asked Daddy, with a sly grin.

40 "Daddy, you are *sooooo busted*!" exclaimed Jack.

41 "Well, I guess we've solved the mystery of the Great Cupcake Heist," said Jaci. "Daddy, you should have been the #1 suspect from the beginning!"

Questions

1. Which word has a similar meaning to *heist* in the title?
    a. recipe
    b. plan
    c. robbery
    d. story

2. Explain how the title uses exaggeration to let us know that this will be a humorous story.

____

____

3. Which word would be the **best** replacement for *scrumptious* in paragraph 4?

  a. good
  b. delectable
  c. tasty
  d. sweet

4. In paragraph 10, if Jaci believes that Jack has stolen one of the cupcakes, why does she say he's *very funny*?

____

5. **Alliteration** is using two or more words in a row which start with the same sound. What phrase in paragraph 13 is an example of alliteration?

____

6. What does *bedecked* mean in paragraph 6?

  a. ready to go
  b. dressed up
  c. on time
  d. in a hurry

7. In paragraph 17, two words are in *italics*. If you were reading the story out loud, how would you read these two words?

____

8. Which word would be a good replacement for *assuredly* in paragraph 22?

  a. possibly
  b. probably
  c. definitely
  d. seemingly

9. In paragraph 23, what does the phrase *a real whodunit* mean?

____

10. Why do you think Mom has a wicked grin on her face in paragraph 23 when she tells the kids they have a whodunit on their hands?

____

11. In paragraph 33, why did Jeff ask if they were going to make him walk the plank, or take his temperature, if he had eaten the cupcake?

____

Anna Beth's Birthday Party

1 "Well, Anna Bee, it's been great talking to you, but I bet it's almost your bedtime, huh?" asked Daddy. Eleven-year-old Anna Beth looked into the computer screen and took a deep breath.

2 "Daddy, what about my birthday? Please tell me you're going to make it home for my party," she implored. Anna Beth's daddy was a Marine. He had been stationed overseas for twenty months and had been due to come home on leave weeks ago. He had thought he would be home in plenty of time for Anna Beth's birthday party, but his orders had not come through yet. Now the party was only one week away and the clock was ticking.

3 "Anna Bee, it doesn't look like it. I'm so sorry, honey; I just don't know what's going on. I put in for leave weeks ago, but I still haven't heard anything," said Daddy.

4 Anna Beth swallowed hard and struggled to hold back the tears she felt welling up in her eyes. "That's OK, Daddy. I understand," she said.

5 Momma put a hand on her shoulder. "You know what? We'll Skype during the party, Anna Bee! You could arrange that, right Daddy?" asked Momma.

6 "Absolutely!" said Daddy, trying his best to sound upbeat. "It will almost be like I'm right there with you, Anna Bee."

7 As Anna Beth walked up the stairs to go to bed, she felt so sad. Through all of Daddy's years in the Marines, he had never missed her birthday. What kind of party would it be if her daddy wasn't there? She fought to keep the tears back again, but this time they wouldn't stop. It just wasn't fair. Momma and Daddy always said that when Anna Beth felt lonely for her daddy, she should try to remember all the good he was accomplishing and all the people he was helping. But tonight Anna Beth didn't care one bit

about any of that. He was her daddy and she wanted him home for her birthday, and that was that.

8 Over the next week, Anna Beth and her mom planned her birthday party. She was having a slumber party with five of her closest friends. First, they would go to Anna Beth's favorite restaurant for dinner, then home for cake, ice cream, games, etc. Then the next day they would all go and have their toenails done at a nail salon.

9 Each night as they planned the party, Anna Beth and her mother talked to Daddy on Skype, but Anna Beth never asked again about him coming home. She knew her daddy wanted desperately to be there for her birthday, and if there were any way he could be there, he would. She knew he already felt terrible about not being able to come, and she didn't want to make him feel any worse. That didn't make it any easier for her, though. As the big day grew closer, Anna Beth felt more and more glum. Every day she came straight home from school and headed to her room to cry. How could she have a birthday without Daddy?

10 On the night of the party, one by one, all her friends arrived. They each brought a sleeping bag, an overnight bag, and a beautifully wrapped present. The house was decorated in Anna Beth's favorite colors and patterns, black and hot pink zebra, and even the cake was decorated to match. Everything was perfect, Anna Beth thought, except for one thing that was missing; one very big thing.

11 Just as the girls were about to leave for the restaurant, there was a knock at the door.

12 "Who can that be, Momma?" asked Anna Beth. "Everyone is here."

13 "I don't know, Anna Bee; why don't you answer the door," said Momma, with a smile.

14 Anna Beth opened the door and couldn't believe her eyes.

15 "Daddy! You made it, I can't believe it! How'd you do it?" cried Anna Beth, hugging him tightly.

16 "My leave orders finally came in three days ago and Momma and I decided to surprise you," said Daddy. "Are you surprised?"

17 "Oh, yes, Daddy! This is going to be the best birthday ever!" said Anna Beth.

Questions

1. Which word is the **best** synonym for *implored* in paragraph 2?
   a. stated
   b. said
   c. implied
   d. pleaded

2. Which word is the **best** synonym for *upbeat* in paragraph 6?
   a. interested
   b. happy
   c. upright
   d. alert

3. Why was Momma smiling in paragraph 13?

___

4. In paragraph 7, what is the root word of *accomplishing*, and what does it mean?

___

5. When Anna Beth decided she didn't care about all the good her dad was accomplishing, or the people he was helping, she just wanted him home for her birthday, was she being selfish? How would you feel in that situation? Explain your answer.

___

Josh's Big Game

1 The alarm sounded and Josh Bradley awoke with a start. This was it, the day he'd been waiting for all year. His heart began to beat more quickly just thinking of the game. The anticipation was making his stomach do flips.

2 Josh's dad appeared in the doorway.

3 "How's my favorite quarterback?" Dad asked.

4 Josh grinned from ear to ear. "Great, Dad! Ready to win the game!"

5 His father laughed. "Easy, Pal. You don't play until 4:00pm. Let's start with breakfast."

6 Today was the conference championship game between Josh's school, Madison Middle School, and its archrival, Hampshire Middle School. Both teams had had great seasons, with Madison's record being 7-1, and Hampshire's 6-2. Josh in no way underestimated their opponent today. No, he knew this game would be a strenuous battle.

7 After what seemed like a never-ending school day, the last bell rang and Josh headed for the locker room. After suiting up, the team gathered around to listen to Coach Adams' final pep talk.

8 "Well, boys, this is it, the championship game," began Coach Adams. "We've had a great season, you're a tremendous bunch of athletes, and a championship win would just be the cherry on top of such a dream season. Let's go out there and play our best, and that trophy will be ours!"

9 The team headed out to the field. Both teams were fired up, fighting for the right to be known as the conference champions. The game was tight all

the way through the first quarter, with each team scoring a touchdown, making the score at the beginning of the second quarter 7-7.

10 It was 3rd down and 6, when Josh dropped back, looking for a receiver. Suddenly, one of the Hawks' tackles burst through the line from the right, headed right for Josh. Josh never saw him coming and, before he knew it, he was on the ground, moaning in pain. When he opened his eyes, he saw stars. He looked toward the sideline, and it looked like everyone was standing on their heads!

11 Josh closed his eyes and tried shaking his head, but the severe pain that ensued took his breath away. He grabbed his head with both hands and lay flat on his back. Within seconds, Coach Adams, the trainer, and the other coaches were circled around him, asking him how he was feeling. After a brief discussion, they assisted Josh in getting to his feet, and they helped him walk to the locker room where the trainer did a quick assessment.

12 "Josh, I think you have a concussion," said Dr. Huff. "Concussions can be very dangerous; I don't think you should go back in."

13 His mom and dad had rushed from the stands to the locker room, and Josh looked to them for support. "Mom, Dad, I *have* to go back in! This is the biggest game of the year!"

14 There was a pause as his parents exchanged glances; then his father spoke. "I'm afraid Dr. Huff's right," said Mr. Bradley. "Josh, your health is the most important thing. There will be other games."

15 Other games? Josh's eyes filled with tears. He lay back on the stretcher and covered his face with his hands. He had let his team down in the most critical game of the year.

16 His parents drove Josh to the hospital. An x-ray showed that Josh had indeed suffered a concussion. Although his head hurt, the pain of missing the game was much worse. As he was lying on the bed, trying desperately

to fight back the tears, he heard a commotion in the hallway. It got louder and louder, but then everything abruptly went quiet. Josh was wondering what was going on out there when suddenly the door flew open and there was Coach Adams and the entire team. The players were laughing and cheering, whooping and hollering, as they piled into his room and gathered 'round his bed.

17 "We did it, Josh! We won! We're the champions!"

18 After the cheers subsided, Coach Adams spoke. "Josh, you did the right thing by taking care of yourself. There will be other big games and you're still a champion," said Coach Adams.

19 At that, the team began to chant, "WE'RE NUMBER 1! WE'RE NUMBER 1! WE'RE NUMBER 1!" Josh smiled in spite of his pain, and he knew then that Coach Adams and his parents had been right. He couldn't wait 'til next year.

Questions

1. Divide the word *anticipation* from paragraph 1 into syllables.

____

2. Which word would be a good substitute for *anticipation* in paragraph 1?
   a. fear
   b. disgust
   c. nervousness
   d. insomnia

3. Who is telling this story?
   a. Josh
   b. Coach Adams
   c. Mr. Bradley
   d. a narrator

4. Which word would be a good substitute for *conference* in paragraph 6?
   a. league
   b. town
   c. important
   d. annual

5. What is the **main** theme of this story?
   a. football is fun but dangerous
   b. you can count on teammates when you're down
   c. people should quit playing football and concentrate on schoolwork
   d. our health is far more important than a football game

6. Divide the word *underestimated* from paragraph 6 into syllables.

____

7. In paragraph 11, what does *ensued* mean?
   a. flowed
   b. jolted
   c. followed
   d. disrupted

8. In paragraph 14, what does it mean when it says that Josh's parents *exchanged glances*?

____

9. Why did Josh's parents exchange glances?

____

10. In paragraph 15, what does *critical* mean?
   a. loud
   b. exciting
   c. important
   d. expensive

11. If someone didn't know what *critical* means, what fact from the story would help them figure it out?

____

12. What would be another good title for this story?
    a. How Josh Hurt His Head
    b. Let's Celebrate!
    c. Football Is a Game of Inches
    d. Josh Learns a Painful Lesson

13. Do you think Josh will play football again next year? Explain your answer.

____

14. What is the name of the football team's trainer?

____

15. Which word does NOT have the same meaning as *commotion* in paragraph 16?
    a. hubbub
    b. conversation
    c. uproar
    d. tumult

Meagan's Trip

1 Meagan Wells watched the last seconds on the clock tick off, and then she ran for the door as the bell sounded. Finally! School was over and the weekend was here.

2 Meagan belongs to a local Girl Scout troop. The girls learn all kinds of cool things like cooking, sewing, and first aid. They also volunteer at a local animal shelter on the weekends, helping find at-risk animals good homes. Meagan really enjoys doing that. In fact, she is thinking of one day becoming a veterinarian.

3 This weekend will be different, though. It's the weekend of their big campout. Instead of the Happy Valley Humane Society, the girls are heading to Mount Ellis, where they will camp out overnight, and then hike to the summit of the big hill on Saturday.

4 Ms. Johnson, their troop leader, will lead the hike. The rest of the girls in Meagan's troop - Kerstyn, Jillian, Sarah, Avery and Lana - are just as excited about the weekend as Meagan.

5 When Meagan's mom drops her off at Ms. Johnson's house, most of the girls are already there, loading their gear into the van.

6 "Hey, Meagan," said Avery.

7 "Hey, Avery. Ready for the campout?" said Meagan.

8 "I sure am. I can't believe it's finally here. We're actually going to climb Mount Ellis!" said Avery.

9 "It seems like we've prepared for this forever," said Kerstyn.

10 "Did everyone remember thick socks?" asked Jillian. "Remember, Ms. Johnson said it's easy to get blisters when we hike as much as we're going to tomorrow."

11 "I brought mine," said Lana

12 "Hi, everybody! We drove by the store to get some extra water. Is everyone ready?" asked Sarah.

13 The girls all climbed into Ms. Johnson's van and headed for the camp site. When they arrived, it was not quite dusk.

14 "OK, girls. Let's get our tents set up quickly, before it gets dark. Then we'll start supper," said Ms. Johnson.

15 The girls had practiced assembling their tents over the last few weeks and their dry runs paid off, as they got them up in no time. They helped Ms. Johnson get the fire going, and then began roasting hot dogs and marshmallows. The food tasted especially good cooked over the open fire. They sat around eating s'mores and telling ghost stories for a while before Ms. Johnson said it was time for bed.

16 "Well, we should probably all turn in. Tomorrow's going to be a fantastic day, but we'll need a good night's sleep and all the energy we possess if we're going to enjoy it."

17 The next morning, the girls packed their tents and backpacks and started the hike. Everything was going swimmingly, until Meagan stopped to take a

picture of some flowers. The others went on ahead, so after she got her shot, Meagan ran along the trail to catch up. She didn't see the root in the trail and tripped and crashed to the ground.

18 "Help," Meagan cried.

19 The girls and Ms. Johnson ran back to see what had happened.

20 "I think your arm is broken, Meagan," said Ms. Johnson. "Avery, Jillian, and Sarah; you stay with Meagan. Kerstyn, Lana, and I will go for help."

21 The three girls all stayed close to Meagan. Her arm hurt, but knowing she was preventing the troop from making the climb hurt even worse. Tears filled her eyes.

22 "Oh, no, is it hurting really bad?" asked Sarah.

23 "Yes," said Meagan. "But mostly I'm just sorry I'm causing everyone to miss out on the hike," said Meagan, tears streaming down her face.

24 "Don't worry," said Avery. "We'll do it another time."

25 Meagan said, "Maybe when Ms. Johnson gets back, you all could go on."

26 "No way!" said Jillian. "We're a team. We all go together, or not at all."

27 Meagan smiled. "Really?" she asked.

28 "Of course," said Sarah. "We wouldn't dream of finishing the climb without you."

29 Meagan was disappointed that they wouldn't make it to the top of Mount Ellis, but that hardly mattered now, because she had discovered just how much her group of friends cared about her.

Questions

1. The title of this story, *Meagan's Trip*, has a double meaning. Explain what those meanings are.

____

____

2. What is the name of the animal shelter where Meagan volunteers on weekends?

____

3. What does *veterinarian* mean?

____

4. Divide veterinarian into syllables.

____

5. Which word means the same thing as *summit* in paragraph 3?
   a. base
   b. peak
   c. side
   d. middle

6. Which two word phrase in paragraph 15 is a synonym for *practice*?

____

7. Which phrase means the same thing as *swimmingly* in paragraph 17?
   a. very well
   b. pretty badly
   c. very fast
   d. not too bad

8. In paragraph 17, what does *shot* mean?

a. flower
b. BB gun
c. photograph
d. rest

9. How was Meagan's falling and breaking her arm related to her stopping to take pictures of the flowers?

____

____

10. To *hinder* someone means to keep them from doing something. What word in paragraph 21 has the same meaning as *hindering*?

____

11. The previous story, *Josh's Big Game*, has some similarities with this story. List at least three.

____

____

12. There is one major difference between *Josh's Big Game* and *Meagan's Trip*. In the first story, after Josh got injured, his friends kept going without him. In the second story, Meagan's friends refused to keep going without her after she broke her arm. Josh's friends on his team cared about him just as much as Meagan's friends from her Girl Scout troop cared about her. So why did they keep playing after Josh had to go to the hospital? Why didn't they refuse to go on until Josh was recovered?

____

____

A Boy and His Best Friend

1 "Here, Chance! C'mon, boy!" Ten-year-old Travis Matthews called to his dog, who came running as soon as he heard his master's voice. The Labrador retriever nearly knocked Travis over as he approached, showering him with soft, wet kisses, as only a dog can do.

2 Ever since he could remember, Travis had wanted a dog to call his very own. Oh, sure, there was the old sheep dog, Ralph. He was a good dog - great at rounding up sheep and even cattle. But Travis wanted his own dog, his own special friend. Because there was so much work to do on the farm, Travis was usually up before dawn doing chores, and being an only child was often lonely. But Ma and Pa wanted Travis to wait until he was old enough to take care of a dog on his own. Then, when he was seven years old, Pa died and Travis had to take on a lot more responsibility around the farm. Then one day something happened that Travis will never forget -- Ma drove the wagon into the yard on her return from town, and the most beautiful puppy he had ever seen jumped out of the back. He was so little that he tumbled a couple of times when he landed.

3 "Ma!" cried Travis, "you got me a dog?"

4 Ma smiled. "Well, I saw him in town. He was the runt of the Perkins' litter and needed a good home. You've been working so hard lately, so I just thought I'd take a chance on this little guy," said Ma.

5 "Thanks, Ma. I mean it, he's perfect," said Travis. He picked up the rambunctious bundle of fur and held him tight.

6 "You're welcome," said Ma. "But, remember -- he's your responsibility. You'll have to take care of him, and you'll still have to stay on top of your chores."

7 "I know, Ma. I promise I'll take good care of him, and I'll still get everything done," said Travis. "Thanks again for taking the chance, Ma."

8 Travis's eyes lit up as he looked at his new puppy. "Hey, that would be a great name! I think I'll call you Chance. Yeah, that's a perfect name for you, little buddy. What do you think?" As he talked, the little puppy's tail wagged vigorously and he covered Travis's face in kisses.

9 Now, a year later, Chance was Travis's shadow. Travis never went anywhere without him. When Travis got up early to get the eggs, Chance went with him. When Travis plowed the field, Chance trotted behind the horses. When Travis walked to school, Chance went with him and sat outside the one-room schoolhouse all day, faithfully waiting for his master. He even slept on the end of Travis's bed. The two were always together.

10 One day, Travis was in the barn laying new hay down for the animals. He accidentally dropped his pitchfork and Eula, the old mare, got spooked. She began bucking and trying to run out of her stall. In her fear and confusion, she trampled over Travis, knocking him out. Chance, sensing that Travis was hurt, ran out of the barn toward the house. He stood on the front porch and began barking.

11 "What is it, boy? Where's Travis?" asked Ma.

12 Chance barked again, then turned and ran toward the barn. He got half way there, and stopped and looked back at Ma. He barked again and ran into the barn. When Ma noticed that Eula was out in the yard, she quickly followed Chance into the barn. She found Travis in Eula's stall, rubbing his forehead.

13 "What happened?" asked Travis.

14 "Well, I'm not sure, but somehow you got knocked out and this little fella started barking to let me know something was wrong. I'm so glad he sticks so close to you. He really the saved the day," said Ma.

15 "Good boy!" said Travis, as he petted the dog's head. "You're the best friend someone could ever hope for!"

16 "Ma, I'm sure glad you took a chance on Chance!"

Questions

1. There are a few clues in the story that let the reader know that it took place a long time ago. List two of those clues.

____

2. In paragraph 6, Ma uses an idiom. What does she mean when she tells Travis he has to *stay on top of* his chores?

____

3. What does the author mean when she says the puppy is *rambunctious* in paragraph 5?

   a. he's dark brown
   b. he is very big for his age
   c. he is excited and won't sit still
   d. he has very droopy eyes

4. What is the six-word metaphor in paragraph 1?

____

5. What is the four-word metaphor in paragraph 9?

____

6. What would be the best word to describe the relationship between Travis and Chance?

   a. frivolous
   b. inseparable
   c. nice
   d. respectable

Zeus vs. Typhon

1 I am Zeus, god of the sky and rain. I live in a wonderful place called Olympus, the land of the gods. I became ruler of the gods after I overthrew my father, Cronus. I have two brothers, Poseidon, god of the sea, and Hades, god of the underworld. After our father's demise, we drew lots to determine who would be the supreme ruler of the gods, and fate was with me that day.

2 My favorite weapon is the mighty thunderbolt. I have been known to hurl this thunderbolt at those who displease me, lie, or do not keep their promises. I despise disloyalty. I represent justice and mercy and I am known as the protector of the weak and the punisher of the wicked.

3 Although I have great power, not all in my kingdom obey me. A people that have given me much grief are the Titans. It all began when Gaia - you might know her as Mother Nature - became angry with me. She is the mother of the Titans and felt as if I had treated her sons unjustly. I am a father myself, so I understood her feelings, but I am Zeus, after all, and must protect my domain and position. However, I feared Gaia, because she is a terrifying foe, and I had no idea what she would do next.

4 I soon found out. Gaia joined forces with Tartarus, a rather nasty, gloomy underworld dweller to create a monster to use to destroy me and become the new ruler of the gods. This monster was horrific. His name was Typhon. This Typhon had amazing powers and frightened us all with his ability to spew great amounts of fire from his very mouth! He attacked our home in Olympus, roaring and throwing flaming rocks at us, setting everything on fire. We all ran for our lives!

5 We fled to Capernea, where we felt that we should disguise ourselves, so we transformed ourselves into animals. We stayed in Capernea for a while, but I soon received word that Athena, the goddess of wisdom, was calling me a coward for running away from Typhon. I thought at great length

about this accusation. At last I decided that Athena was right: I must summon the courage to confront this monster, Typhon.

6 I gathered up my weapons, thunder and lightning, and set out to find Typhon. When I found him, I immediately blasted him with the biggest lightning bolt I had. Typhon was stunned and momentarily left in a daze. I hurriedly challenged him to a hand-to-hand fight, believing that I had the upper hand. What I was unaware of was that this Typhon had two hundred knives in his mouth! All at once, he unleashed these knives at me. I dodged as many as possible, but, alas, my fingers and toes were cut off. I was helpless to defend myself. Typhon took me to the Corycian Cave, on the side of Mount Parnassus. He left his half-beast, half-girl sister, Delphyne, to guard me.

7 Suddenly, my son Hermes and his friend Aegipan appeared in the cave. They quickly and cleverly reattached all of my fingers and toes. My strength was restored to me at once! I knew just what I must do. I gathered up my thunderbolts, hitched up Nadar, my winged horse, to my chariot, and roared out of the heavens, looking for Typhon. Upon finding him, I chased him into Sicily, hurling thunderbolts at him. When we reached Sicily, I grabbed Mount Aetna and threw it on top of Typhon. And he has never been heard from since that day.

Questions

1. What information in paragraph 1 lets us know that Zeus is ruler of the gods?

____

2. Zeus is a mythical character whose home is the mythical Mt. Olympus. Which of these places is NOT mythical?

 a. the Land of Oz
 b. the Great Smoky Mountains
 c. the Land of Narnia
 d. Big Rock Candy Mountain

3. Divide disguise into syllables.

____

4. When Zeus and his friends transformed themselves into animals, that was a kind of:

   a. exploration
   b. shift
   c. metamorphosis
   d. growth

5. What would be a good synonym for *demise* in paragraph 1?

   a. downfall
   b. gift
   c. blessing
   d. announcement

6. List at least three things in this story that show that it's not a true story.

____

7. What clue does this story give us about Athena that would explain why she's usually right?

____

8. Who helped Gaia create Typhon?

____

9. In paragraph 6, which word means almost the same thing as *temporarily*?

____

10. Which word or phrase is closest to the meaning of *despise* in paragraph 2?

   a. abhor
   b. dislike
   c. look down on
   d. take a dim view of

Jack's First Christmas in Africa

1 "Hi, Jack," said Mom. "How was your day?"

2 "Fine, I guess," sighed ten-year-old Jack.

3 "Is everything alright? You don't sound very convincing."

4 "Yes, Mom, everything's fine."

5 Really, though, Jack wasn't fine. He was homesick. He and his parents had moved to Africa six months earlier to be missionaries. Africa was very different than America, but most of the time Jack was happy. He had made friends at the school and he was getting used to the bizarre food, and even living in a hut had become tolerable. But now it was close to Christmas, and Jack missed America more than ever.

6 Some of the African people didn't even celebrate Christmas, and even the ones who did had very different traditions. There were no authentic Christmas trees, no ornaments, and definitely no snow. He wouldn't be enjoying any of his mom's special Christmas cookies because there was no way to get the ingredients she would need to bake them. And just what kind of present did Jack expect to get? No new video games, no new skateboard, no new toys at all. None of these things were available in the little village in the middle of the African jungle.

7 Then, one day at school, their class began talking about Christmas.

8 "Tell us, Jack. How do you celebrate Christmas in America," said Wahid.

9 "Well, first we put up a Christmas tree in our home."

10 "A Christmas tree?" asked Jalil. "I have never heard of such a thing."

11 "It's an evergreen tree, one that never loses its leaves. We hang all sorts of decorations all over it, even lights," said Jack.

12 The African children listened in amazement to all that Jack had to share about Christmas in America. He told them about all the great food they ate, about wrapping presents for his parents in beautiful red, green, silver, and gold paper. He told them about all the family get-togethers, the caroling on the cold winter nights, and the stockings filled with candy and all kinds of treats. He even told them about the special candlelight service they always attended on Christmas Eve.

13 "Christmas is really about giving, and spending time with friends and family," said Jack.

14 Finally, a week later, it was the last day of school before the Christmas holidays would start. Jack moved extra slow when he awoke, wishing more than ever he could just stay in his bed. He didn't want to celebrate Christmas in Africa. It just wasn't the same. He dreaded going to school, but he knew he had no choice.

15 When Jack walked into his classroom, he couldn't believe his eyes. There before him was a Christmas tree! It wasn't the kind of tree he had in America, but it was a tree, covered in decorations, homemade versions of the ones Jack had described to his class. There were presents under the tree wrapped in paper that had been painted. The colors were red and green with accents of gold and silver. On the table there were several dozen special African cookies, along with some punch. The students had even cut up tiny pieces of paper and strewn it all over the floor to look like snow.

16 "Surprise, Jack!" said Wahid. "We wanted to bring American Christmas to you here in Africa."

17 "Yes," said Jalil. "We know you miss your home, but we are glad you are here to celebrate Christmas with us this year."

18 "Open your present, Jack," said Ourja.

19 Jack tore the paper off the present and found a mitt and ball for playing a native African stick game.

20 Jack smiled. "Thanks, guys," said Jack. "It looks like it's going to be a merry Christmas after all!"

Questions

1. What were two of the biggest adjustments Jack had to make when he moved to Africa?

____

2. Divide *amazement* into syllables.

____

3. In paragraph 3, what did Jack's mother mean when she said he didn't sound very convincing?

____

4. What clues does Jack give his mother that made her say that?

____

5. Which word would NOT be a good synonym for *bizarre* in paragraph 5?
   a. strange
   b. exotic
   c. boring
   d. weird

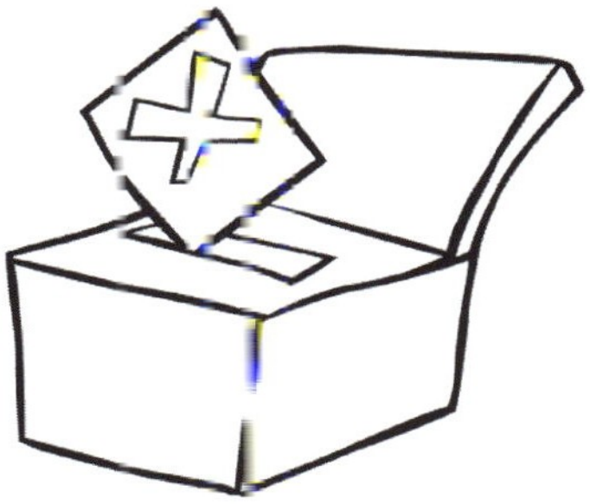

The Big 6th Grade Election

1 "Guess what?" asked twelve-year-old Blake Miller.

2 "What?" asked Mom.

3 "I've decided I'm going to run for 6th grade class president."

4 "That's great, Blake! When is the election?"

5 "Next Friday," said Blake. "I need to start campaigning. Reed said he thinks I'll make a great president and he's going to help me make posters."

6 "What's your platform going to be?" asked Dad.

7 "What do you mean?" asked Blake.

8 "Well, if you're going to run for an office like president, you have to have a platform. A platform is a list of things that you will do for your classmates if you're elected," said Dad.

9 "Hmm," said Blake. "I hadn't really thought about that."

10 "Well," said Mom, "what are some changes you would like to see take place at school? That's a good place to start."

11 "I know!" said Blake. "No more homework!"

12 Dad laughed. "Do you really think Mrs. Sanders is going to agree with that change?" asked Dad.

13 "Probably not," said Blake.

14 "Then it's probably not a good thing to try for," said Mom. "You need to focus on changes that you have a good chance of getting done."

15 "How about two more minutes between classes?" asked Blake. "There's hardly enough time now to get to our classes before they start."

16 "That's a good idea, Blake. Start with that," said Dad.

17 The next day when Blake walked into his homeroom, he noticed a group of students gathered around his friend Reed's desk. When he walked up, he saw that Reed was passing out buttons. Blake smiled, what a great friend, he thought. Then, to his surprise, he saw the buttons didn't say "Vote for Blake"; they said "Vote for Reed."

18 Reed looked sheepishly at Blake. "I'm sorry, Blake. I decided I wanted to run for president, too," said Reed, putting the buttons away.

19 Blake was stunned. Reed was Blake's best friend and yesterday had said that he thought Blake would make a good president. Now he was his opponent.

20 The rest of the school day was weird. Reed didn't sit by him at lunch and some of the kids that usually sat with the two of them decided to sit with Reed. Blake was really worried. He hadn't planned on things turning out this way. Plus, it looked like he was going to have to make his posters all by himself.

21 The next day, Blake got to school early to hang his posters in the hallway. When he arrived, he noticed that today, Reed was passing out chocolate bars with "Reed for President" on the wrapper. Blake felt discouraged, but kept talking to as many friends as he could about his platform ideas.

22 On the day of the election, Mrs. Sanders let the two candidates make a speech. Reed went first.

23 "If I am elected class president, I promise to get an ice cream machine in the cafeteria, have longer recess and make sure we don't have tests on Mondays," said Reed. Everyone cheered.

24 Blake panicked. Ice cream? Longer recess? He was in trouble. His platform wasn't nearly as cool as Reed's. He wondered if he should just throw in the towel right then and there.

25 "Your turn, Blake," said Mrs. Sanders.

26 Blake decided he wouldn't give up, so he stood up and took a deep breath. "If I am elected president, I will ask for two more minutes between classes, I will set up a morning each week before school for help with homework, and I will ask for one extra science field trip each year," said Blake.

27 At the end of the day the votes were tallied, and the principal announced the results over the intercom. Blake couldn't believe it-he was the winner! It was the second time this week he'd felt stunned. As he was leaving school, Reed called out to Blake.

28 "Still friends?" asked Reed.

29 "Sure," said Blake.

30 "Your platform was much more realistic than mine. You will definitely make the best president," said Reed.

Questions

1. Which word in paragraph 27 means *counted*?

____

2. In paragraph 18 we see that *Reed looked sheepishly at Blake*. The word *sheepishly* is an adverb, which means in a sheepish manner. Which word means almost the same thing as *sheepish*?

a. defiant
b. confused
c. embarrassed
d. angry

3. In paragraph 24, what is the four-word idiom, or figure of speech?

____

4. What does the figure of speech mean?

____

5. Which candidate did you think would win the election? Give reasons for your answer.

____

____

Reading: Informational Text

Gabby Douglas: Star of the Olympics

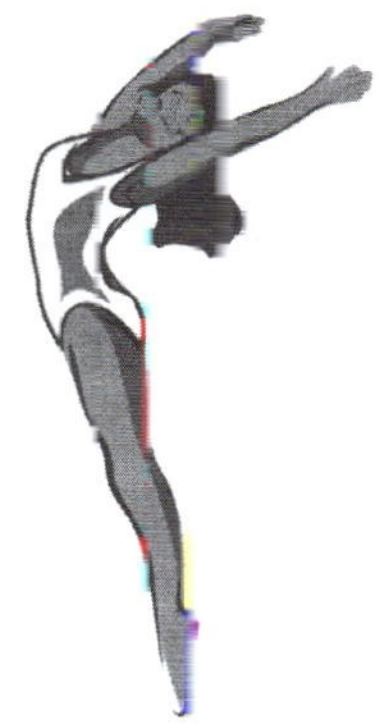

1 She stands at the chalk bowl, whitening her hands, her determined face staring at the uneven bars. She moves to the bars, salutes the judges, and mounts. Over the next few minutes she performs an almost perfect routine, hailed by some experts as one of the most amazing performances by anyone at the 2012 Olympic Games. She moves through each maneuver of the routine with the confidence of a mature competitor, while the watching world holds its collective breath. As she sticks her dismount, she flashes that beautiful, contagious smile and we jump out of our seats, cheering. She's done it again!

2 Gabby Douglas arrived at the 2012 Olympic Games in London, England as an underdog, but left the competition as not only a world champion, but also America's sweetheart. The 4'11" 16-year-old young lady mesmerized the world with her power, flexibility, and form. Many who were familiar with her career were concerned that Gabby would crack emotionally under the great pressure of participating in the world's most prestigious athletic event, but her nerves appeared to be made of steel. Even in the most intense moments of the competition, Gabby seemed focused and calm, ready to help Team America bring home the gold. Not only is she the first African-American female to win gold in the individual all-around event, but she has also been nicknamed "Flying Squirrel" because of the way she seems to fly through the air when competing on the bars.

3 Gabby, born on December 31, 1995 in Virginia Beach, Virginia, began her formal gymnastics training at the age of 6 years old. By the time she was 8 years old, she had won a state championship. So, when Gabby turned 14, she left her hometown and family to move to West Des Moines, Iowa, to train with Liang Chow, a trainer known all over the world for turning American gymnasts into Olympic champions and gold medalists. Travis and

Missy Parton, who have a daughter who is also a student of Chow's, offered to be Gabby's host family. Gabby very quickly became close to the Parton family and even considers herself to be a "big sister" to the Parton's four daughters.

4 Leaving her home and family was difficult for Douglas, but would soon prove to be a strategic move. In 2010 at the Nastia Liuken SuperGirl Cup, Gabby made her debut on the national level, winning fourth all-around. She continued to compete throughout the rest of 2010, winning fifth all-around at the 2010 Pan American Championships, earning her a place on the U.S. team. In 2011, the U.S. team won the gold medal in the team finals at the World Artistic Gymnastics Championships in Tokyo, Japan. When she won the 2012 Olympic Trials, in San Jose, California, Gabby earned a place on the U.S. national team that would represent the United States at the 2012 Summer Olympics in London.

5 During the London Olympics, Gabby stood out as a star, not only with her gymnastic skills, but also for her fun personality and support of the other members of the U.S. team. She has become the center of media attention since the Olympics, appearing on the cover of several magazines, such as *Sports Illustrated* and *Time.* She has since been named Sportswoman of the Year by the Women's Sports Foundation and has received several endorsement deals with companies such as Kellogg's and Procter & Gamble.

6 For Gabby, it's all been about a dream. "I think when you have a dream, you won't let anyone stop you," she said. And her dream has definitely come true.

Questions

1. According to this article, what is the most prestigious athletic event in the world?

____

2. Which word is NOT a good synonym for *prestigious*?

a. illustrious
b. distinguished
c. televised
d. respected

3. Is it a fact or opinion that this is the most prestigious athletic event in the world? Explain your answer.

____

____

4. In paragraph 1, which word means "spreading from one person to another"?

____

5. What is a *host family*?

____

6. Which two-word phrase in paragraph 5 refers to agreements Gabby Douglas has made to promote various products and services in exchange for money?

____

7. How many years did it take Gabby to go from her first gymnastics training to winning an Olympic gold medal?

____

8. Which word in paragraph 1 means "movement or series of movements requiring great skill"?

____

9. After reading this article, which of these do you think the author believes was the most important factor in Gabby Douglas's success?

a. her charming personality
b. her natural talent
c. her years of training
d. her host family in Iowa

10. What does *underdog* mean in paragraph 2?

a. the member of a team who has to carry all the bags & run errands, etc.
b. someone who is disliked by most people
c. a very short person
d. someone who isn't expected to win

Gabby Douglas: My Story *

1 Hi, I'm Gabby Douglas. I was a member of the U.S. Women's Gymnastics team in the 2012 Olympic Games. Competing in the Olympics was the most amazing time in my whole life. And, to top it all off, I won the gold medal in the individual all-around event! That's the part you know, but there's much more to my story.

2 When I was young, my big sister took gymnastics. She was always doing cartwheels and turning flips. So I started trying to do the same things I saw her do. And, I was pretty good at it. I could turn a perfect cartwheel by the time I was three years old.

3 So, when I turned six years old, my mom put me in gymnastics, too. By the time I was eight years old, I won the state championship for my age group in Virginia!

4 Anyway, I kept training, kept working hard, and kept winning. I have been so blessed with great coaches, a super supportive mom and sister, and many other people who saw that I had talent and encouraged me to chase my dream. But when I turned fourteen years old, I had to make a very hard, but very important, decision.

5 My coaches and my mom knew that the Olympics in London, England were coming in 2012. They really believed that I had a shot at making the team. I wanted to make that team so badly, more than anything else in the

world! I dreamed about it when I slept, I thought about it all day - at school, practice, no matter where I was. It was my absolute dream.

6 The problem was I needed to go to the next level. Basically, I needed to leave home and go train with another coach who knew what it took to be an Olympic gymnast. It was such a hard decision! I didn't want to be apart from my mom and sister, but I did want to go to the Olympics. Finally, after much thinking, talking, and tears, I decided to go for it.

7 I left my home in Virginia Beach, Virginia and went to live in Des Moines, Iowa to train with Liang Chow, a coach who trained people like Shawn Johnson! Can you believe it? Little old me, training with a world renowned coach! I started living with a wonderful family, the Parton's. They have four daughters of their own, and one of them studied with Coach Chow, too. Travis and Misty treated me just like their very own daughter and I felt like their daughters were my little sisters. I really enjoyed studying with Coach Chow, too. He really helped me sharpen my skills as a gymnast.

8 It was hard, though. There were times when I just wanted to quit and go home. But during those times, Travis and Missy, my mom, and Coach Chow would listen to me, and then gently remind me of my dream. And I'd dry my tears and keep going.

9 Then I made the U.S Women's Gymnastics team at the 2012 Olympic Trials in San Jose, California. I was going to the Olympics! My dream was coming true. When I got to the Olympics, the pressure was crazy. But, I stayed calm and believed in myself, just as I'd been trained to do. And, as they say, "The rest is history!"

10 So, I ask you: what's your dream? Whatever it is, go for it! Live it, breathe it, and work really hard. And just like me, your dream can come true, too!

**This story wasn't actually written by Gabby Douglas. It's a biographical work based on her life.*

Questions

1. Imagine that you asked Gabby "Do you think you would have become an Olympic gold medalist in gymnastics if it weren't for your big sister?" What do you think she would say? Explain your answer.

____

____

2. According to this article, what person played the greatest part in helping Gabby become an Olympic champion?

____

3. Gabby says she sometimes wanted to give up her dream and move back to Virginia. Why do you think she sometimes felt like that? Give at least two reasons.

____

____

4. The previous story about Gabby was written in the third person. This one is written in the first person. Which one helps you have a better understanding of Gabby Douglas as a person? Explain your answer.

____

____

5. After reading this article, which word would you say best describes Gabby Douglas?

a. modest
b. arrogant
c. lucky
d. vain

The Wonderful World of World Records

1 Have you ever thought about just how many world records exist? A lot of people know only about world records in athletics, but, actually, there are thousands and thousands of different types of world records, in just about any area you can envision.

2 Take Edward Watson's dog, Rose: in 2010, Rose set a world record by being able to catch seven Frisbees, thrown one at a time, and holding all seven in her mouth. So, she holds the Guinness World Record for "Most Discs Caught and Held in the Mouth by a Dog." Good girl, Rose.

3 Next, there's Maze Restaurant, in the United Kingdom. This restaurant holds the world record for the "Most Expensive Pizza." This extraordinary pizza comes with thin crust, an onion sauce, white truffle paste, fontina cheese, mozzarella cheese, pancetta, mushrooms, lettuce, and shavings from a very rare Italian white truffle. Depending on the price and amount of truffles used, this pizza normally sells for $178 US dollars. That costs more than some families pay for a whole week of groceries!

4 Did you know that there are many children who are record holders? There's Ethan Cain, who set a world record for being the youngest plate spinner in 2004, when he was only 21 months old. In order to obtain the

record, Ethan had to perform several tricks with the plate while it was spinning. Serena Henne became the youngest person to put together the Lego London Tower Bridge, at just six years, eleven months, and twenty-seven days old. Another youthful record holder is Poorvie Choudhary, who in 2011 became the youngest person to recite all 118 elements of the Periodic Table correctly with their symbols. Then, in March of 2012, five-year-old Brawley Jacobs set the record for being the youngest person to bowl over 100 points, with no bumpers on the lanes or outside assistance.

5 In 2011, Emily McManaman set the record for being the fastest four-year-old to paint a rainbow. Emily had to use all the colors of the rainbow, and she painted it in 1 minute and 5.52 seconds. Finally, on a more serious note, Cooper Bayne, from Austin, Texas, became the youngest child to shave his head in support of the many people battling cancer. He was only 2,035 days old when he accomplished this feat, which is about five-and-a-half years old.

6 There are several places you can go to learn more about world records. The most famous authority on world records, hands down, is The Guinness Book of World Records. It's an actual book you can buy, with a new, updated edition published every year. These days, of course, the company also has a website, www.guinnessworldrecords.com. Another site devoted to world records is www.recordsetter.com, which focuses on records created and held by kids. The site also provides guidelines to follow if you want to create your own world record attempt.

7 Really, a world record can be in almost anything. There are records held for balancing on one leg, the most hula hoop spins, the largest group of kazoo players, etc. The list goes on and on. You name it, and there's probably a world record holder for it, even if it's frivolous. So, what's your special talent? What can you do really well, for a long time, or differently than anyone else you know? Whatever it is, you just might be able to turn it into a world record!

Questions

1. What word in paragraph one is a synonym for *sports*?

____

2. Why do you think Guinness comes out with a new edition of their book of world records every year?

____

3. Which word is closest in meaning to *frivolous* in paragraph 7?
   a. serious
   b. trivial
   c. important
   d. monumental

4. Consider two of the world records mentioned in this article: hula hoop spinning, and the largest group of kazoo players. Would you consider these to be frivolous world records? Explain your answer.

____

____

5. What is the main theme of this article?
   a. there are many different kinds of world records
   b. most world records are silly
   c. children hold most of the current world records
   d. anyone can set a world record

All About New Zealand

1 Down in the southern hemisphere, not too far from the South Pole is a tiny country called New Zealand. New Zealand is made up of two separate islands, known as the North Island and the South Island.

2 About a millennium ago, New Zealand's native people, the Maori, arrived in New Zealand from a place they call Hawaiki, and they lived on the islands by themselves for hundreds of years. In 1840, New Zealand became a colony of Great Britain when an agreement called the Treaty of Waitangi was signed between the British and the Maori. This treaty is known as the founding document of New Zealand. New Zealand remains a British colony today.

3 New Zealand is a small country, only about the size of Colorado or Japan. Its population is only four million people, so it is not as crowded as many other areas in the world. In New Zealand, you can find any kind of landscape you are looking for. There are beautiful mountains, lush

rainforests, and open fields. Looming volcanoes and stunning beaches overlook the Pacific Ocean. The weather in New Zealand is very mild most of the time, with the average temperature at 68-86 degrees Fahrenheit. The North Island's climate is more sub-tropical, while the South Island's weather is clear and brisk. This climate makes New Zealand an ideal place for vacationing and holidays.

4 Each morning, the sun rises first for New Zealanders, because of the country's location on the earth. This places New Zealand's time zone twelve hours ahead of Greenwich Mean Time. So, if you visit New Zealand, you will cross over the dateline and lose a day altogether during travel.

5 Most of the goods and supplies the people use must be imported, or shipped into New Zealand. This fact makes some things very expensive there, including fuel and certain grocery items. New Zealand leaders are also very strict about what is brought into the country by tourists. Even now, a thousand years after New Zealand's first people settled there, the country does not have any snakes or pesky insects, such as mosquitoes, anywhere on either island.

6 The country's capital, Wellington, is located on the southern tip of the North Island. Wellington is a metropolis, or large, busy city, full of the sights and sounds you'd expect to find in any city of its size. New Zealand's cultural museum, Te Papa, is located in Wellington. Inside you can see exhibits showing the Maori people, the history of New Zealand, native animals of New Zealand and much more.

7 While visiting New Zealand, you will never run out of things to do and see. If you like ocean life, you could go on a whale watching cruise, where you might spot several whales and be entertained by hundreds of dolphins. If you like winter sports, you might climb to the top of Mount Ruapehu or Mount Whakapapa and ski in soft, powder-like drifts of snow. You can experience breathtaking sights such as Lake Taupo, New Zealand's largest lake, and eat some of the best chocolate in the world at the New Zealand branch of Cadbury. You can even swim in the middle of winter, thanks to

the many hot spring baths formed by New Zealand's several active volcanoes. New Zealand is also the filming location for several of your favorite movies, such as *The Lord of the Rings* series and *The Chronicles of Narnia* series. The attraction list is endless.

8 So, the next time your family is looking for a place to vacation, steer them toward New Zealand. It could be the trip of a lifetime.

Questions

1. What is the name of New Zealand's largest lake?

____

2. Which of these would be considered an American *metropolis*?
   a. the Rocky Mountains
   b. Yellowstone National Park
   c. New York City
   d. the National Football League

3. Is New Zealand close to the United States? Explain your answer.

____

4. Which American state has a name very similar to the name of the ancient homeland of the Maori people, before they arrived in New Zealand?

____

5. Which phrase could replace the word *millennium* in paragraph 1?
   a. a hundred years
   b. a thousand years
   c. five hundred years
   d. two hundred and fifty years

Earthquakes and Volcanoes in New Zealand

1 Of the many interesting things about New Zealand, perhaps its geological activity ranks near the top of the list. In New Zealand you find high mountains, active volcanoes, and many earthquakes. This is due to the fact that New Zealand lies on the boundary of the Australian and Pacific Plates. These plates are pieces of the earth's crust. The Pacific Plate lies under the Pacific Ocean, while the Australian Plate lies under Australia. This location is responsible for the unique geological make-up of New Zealand.

2 Upon visiting New Zealand, be prepared to experience an earthquake. Earthquakes happen when there is a sudden burst of energy released at the Earth's crust which is deep within the Earth. This energy causes the Earth to send off seismic waves, which in turn cause the ground to shake and even crack. The deeper the quake, the less damage will be seen on the surface. The shallower the quake, the more surface damage is done.

3 New Zealand, nicknamed "Shaky Isles," has about 20,000 earthquakes recorded each year, most so minor that they are not felt. The country has about 200 earthquakes yearly that are big enough to be felt and cause damage. The largest New Zealand city that is most susceptible to earthquakes is the capitol city of Wellington. The most recent devastating earthquake in New Zealand occurred in Christchurch at Canterbury in February of 2011. This earthquake was a 6.4 on the Richter, or

measurement scale and caused 185 deaths. The structural damage to the city was great and Christchurch is still trying to recover.

4 Below is a table showing ten of New Zealand's largest earthquakes.

Date	Location	Region	Magnitude	Depth	Latitude	Longitude	Deaths
1-23-1855	Lake Wairarapa	Lake Wairarapa	8.2	33 km	41.198 S	175.20 E	9
1826	Fiordland	South Island	8.0	25 km	44.99 S	167.00 E	
1460	Wellington Region	Wellington	8.0	25 km	41.39 S	174.80 E	
9-14-1959	Raoul Island	Kermadec Islands	7.8	35 km	28,.82 S	177.07 W	
6-16-2006	Raoul Island	Kermadec Islands	7.6	33 km	31.56 S	179.30 W	
7-8-1843	Toaroa Junction	Manawatu	7.6	12 km	39.59 S	176.20 E	2
10-14-1848	Blenheim	Marlborough	7.4	12 km	41.89 S	173.60 E	3
2-3-1931	North of Napier	Hawke's Bay	7.4	20 km	39.29 S	177.00 E	256
2-13-1931	East of Napier	Hawke's Bay	7.3	30 km	39.55 S	177.31 E	
3-5-1934	Pahiatua	Manawatu	7.2	12 km	40.54 S	176.29 E	2

5 New Zealand is also known for its active volcanoes. An active volcano is a volcano that has erupted in the past 600 years. When a volcano erupts, it spews lava, an extremely hot liquid formed from volcanic gases, volcanic glass and crystals. New Zealand has three active volcanoes: Ruapehu, Ngauruhoe and Tongariro.

6 Ruapehu, at 9,175 feet is the highest peak on the North Island of New Zealand and carries its only permanent snowfield. Within this snowfield is a hot crater lake. Since 1889, over twelve steam eruptions `and four ash eruptions have been recorded.

7 Ngauruhoe, at 7,504 feet was first spotted in 1839 and since then there have been sixty recorded eruptions. There have been several instances of lava flow, including the years 1870, 1949 and seventeen instances in 1954. Some of this lava flow followed hot avalanches, or falling snow.

8 Tongariro, at 6,458 feet is actually a multiple volcano, with several craters, or large holes, within a summit of three miles in diameter. Four of these have erupted over the course of history.

9 As you can see, the people of New Zealand live with the knowledge that at any time they could experience a powerful earthquake or volcano.

Questions

1. The previous article encouraged people to visit New Zealand. Would this article make the average person in America more likely or less likely to want to visit New Zealand? Explain your answer.

____

____

2. From the table of the ten most powerful earthquakes in New Zealand's history, in what year did the most recent one occur?

____

3. On what date did the earthquake that killed 256 people take place?

____

4. How deep was this earthquake?

____

5. This article says New Zealand has over 200 earthquakes a year which are powerful enough to be felt. Why do you think the previous article about New Zealand didn't mention this fact?

____

____

Metamorphosis

1 Have you ever heard the word "metamorphosis?" Metamorphosis is a scientific word that basically means to completely change.

2 There are several different uses for the word metamorphosis, but it normally describes a process that many insects go through when growing from being an infant into an adult. Probably the insects we think of most often when we think of metamorphosis are the butterfly and the moth. In this instance, metamorphosis has four different phases: 1) egg, 2) larva, 3) pupa, and 4) adult.

3 All butterflies and moths begin life as an egg. Depending on the species of butterfly or moth, these eggs can be laid in the spring, summer or fall. Female butterflies and moths lay many tiny eggs at once on leaves. Once the eggs hatch into caterpillars, the caterpillars will eat these same leaves.

4 In the larva (or caterpillar) phase, the caterpillar has one main job: to eat, eat, eat! The caterpillar will eat so much that it can grow 100 times bigger than its starting size in about three weeks. During this feeding frenzy, the caterpillar will shed its skin four or five times before this phase is complete. Some of the food the caterpillar eats will be stored and used later in its life cycle. This phase usually lasts several weeks.

5 In the third, or pupa phase, something very interesting happens. This phase starts when the full grown caterpillar stops eating and turns into a pupa. In the case of butterflies and moths, a pupa is called a chrysalis. The creature becomes very still; if you came across one you would probably think it was dead. Depending on the species, you can find these pupas

hanging from a tree branch, hidden in leaves, or even buried in the ground. Sometimes moths spin a cocoon of silk around the pupa to protect it during this phase. The pupas are often shaped like the letter "J" and this phase can last anywhere from a few weeks to months. Even though it looks like the pupa is just hanging there or even that maybe the insect is dead, the opposite is true - this little bug is going through many astounding changes!

6 In the final or adult phase, the little chrysalis bursts open and out pops a full grown insect, such as a beautiful butterfly. The butterfly now looks very different than it did throughout any of its other stages. It now has two wings, two antennae, two legs and three body parts. Now, the insect can fly. Many adult butterflies and moths only live a couple of weeks, long enough for the females to lay eggs, but some butterflies, like the monarch, hibernate during the winter and can actually live several months.

7 While butterflies and moths may be the insects most people think of that undergo complete metamorphosis, there are several others that go through this amazing process. Some of these insects include beetles, flies, ants, bees, wasps, and fleas.

8 Other insects go through what is called incomplete metamorphosis. Incomplete metamorphosis is different from complete metamorphosis in that these insects do not go through the pupal, or third stage of complete metamorphosis. The three phases of incomplete metamorphosis include 1) egg, 2) nymph, and 3) adult. In the nymph stage, instead of the insect becoming a caterpillar, the nymph is a smaller version of the adult insect without its wings. The insect then becomes an adult by shedding its outer skeleton and developing wings. Some of the insects that undergo incomplete metamorphosis include crickets, grasshoppers, cockroaches and stinkbugs.

9 Metamorphosis is just one of Mother Nature's amazing processes. Look around and see what other fascinating things you can find.

Questions

1. Complete metamorphosis has more stages than incomplete metamorphosis. How many more?

____

2. Does the larva stage occur in both complete and incomplete metamorphosis?

Yes
No

3. Which word would be a good synonym for *frenzy* in paragraph 4?

a. period
b. mania
c. friendly
d. phase

4. When caterpillars are born, what do they use for food?

____

5. According to this article, do pigs undergo metamorphosis, either complete or incomplete?

Yes
No

6. What is another word for chrysalis, according to this article?

____

7. Divide chrysalis into syllables.

____

8. What is one kind of butterfly that hibernates and lives for several months?

____

9. Which word would be the best synonym for *processes* in paragraph 9?
   a. recesses
   b. methods
   c. progresses
   d. results

10. Divide *fascinating* into syllables.

____

11. What is the name of the protective covering made of silk a chrysalis is wrapped in?

____

12. When a baby goes from crawling to walking, is this an example of metamorphosis? Explain your answer.

____

____

How to Make Spaghetti

1 Do you know how to cook? Cooking is not only a great thing to know how to do, but it can also be lots of fun.

2 The most important thing about cooking is following a good recipe. In a recipe you will find everything you need to know in order to make your cooking experience, and your dish itself, successful.

3 In a recipe you will find all the ingredients needed and their measurements. It's very important to pay close attention to the ingredients and the measurements so that the dish you are making will turn out right. Small errors, such as putting three *tablespoons* of salt instead of three *teaspoons* of salt can ruin dishes.

4 You will also find directions for actually making the dish in your recipe. These directions are usually given in step-by-step fashion. Again, you want to make sure you follow each step exactly the way it is given and in the right order.

5 Finally, you can also find the temperature at which to cook your dish, how long to cook it, and how many servings it will provide. A recipe can be altered to accommodate your serving needs. For instance, if you only need to serve four people and your recipe states that the dish will serve eight people, you can cut all of your measurements in half. Or, if your recipe states that the dish will serve four people and you need to serve eight, you can double all the measurements. So, cooking does call for some math skills. Also, it's important to know your oven and stove top. Does your oven cook hotter than the actual temperature says? If so, drop the temperature down twenty-five degrees or lessen the cooking time.

6 Really, cooking isn't hard at all. You just need to be able to follow a good recipe. Try following this recipe; you'll love it!

Spaghetti with Meat Sauce
Ingredients:
1-1.5 lbs. ground beef
½ C onion, finely chopped
1 teaspoon salt
1 teaspoon pepper
1 jar spaghetti sauce
1 package spaghetti
Parmesan cheese, optional

Directions:
Step 1: Using a skillet, season ground beef with salt and pepper, then cook on medium-high with onion on the stove top. Cook meat until it is brown in color, then drain off grease in a colander.

Step 2: When meat is browned, pour the jar of spaghetti sauce over the meat and mix well. Simmer, or cook on low temperature.

Step 3: While meat is cooking, fill a large pot with four to six cups of water. Bring the water to a boil on the stove top over high heat. When the water comes to a rolling boil, or when the water is bubbling up, add spaghetti. Boil spaghetti on high for nine to eleven minutes or until it is tender. Drain water in a colander.

Step 4: Pour meat sauce over spaghetti and mix well. (Many people like to serve this with Parmesan cheese sprinkled over top, but some don't. It's entirely up to you.)

Questions

1. What does optional mean?

____

2. What is the most important thing when it comes to cooking?

____

3. Which word is a good synonym for *altered* in paragraph 5?
   a. changed
   b. doubled
   c. questioned
   d. canceled

4. In Step 1 and Step 3, the author uses the word *colander*, which you may not be familiar with. Look up the definition and write it in the blank space.

____

5. The first sentence in paragraph 5 says this about recipes: *Finally, you can also find the temperature at which to cook your dish, how long to cook it, and how many servings it will provide*. However, in the spaghetti recipe shown, one of these items is missing. Which one?

____

Weather Can Be Dangerous

1 Have you ever thought about just how powerful the weather can be? Well, for starters, consider this: weather helps you decide what to wear each day, what activities to participate in, and even when and if to travel.

2 Think about your clothing. If the weather is going to be warm, you would probably dress in short sleeves. But, if it's going to be cooler, you'd probably grab a jacket on your way out. If it's going to be rainy, you shouldn't wear your favorite shoes. And how about your daily activities? Would you go snow skiing in the middle of summer? Or swimming during a snow storm? And how often do we hear of flights being canceled due to weather?

3 At times, though, there is much more to the weather than deciding what shirt to wear. Weather can be destructive, dangerous and deadly.

4 Has it ever flooded in your area? According to statistics from flood experts, flooding occurs in all fifty states. It is the number one natural disaster in the country and accounts for about seventy deaths per year

across America. Flash floods can produce masses of water ten to twenty feet high. However, it doesn't take ten or twenty feet of water to be dangerous. In fact, just a few feet of water can easily sweep a car away, and a few inches of water can cause major damage to your home.

5 A hurricane is another kind of natural disaster that can have staggering effects on people and their lives. The weather service began recording hurricanes in 1854 and continues to record them today. Hurricanes are destructive storms that begin over the ocean, but often move over the land. They are marked by their vicious winds of 70 miles per hour or higher and torrential rains that can last for days. These terrible storms can cause flooding and power outages and can contaminate a city's drinking water. One of the worst hurricanes in history, known as "The Great Storm of 1900," hit Galveston Island, Texas on September 8, 1900. This horrible storm was responsible for over 6,000 deaths.

6 In many parts of the United States, blizzards can cause big problems. A blizzard is defined as a storm with driving snow, strong winds and intense cold. These storms usually last for a prolonged time and affect a wide area. Blizzards can cause power outages, plumbing problems, and hazards from downed power lines. They can make driving, or even leaving your house, impossible. The extreme temperatures during a blizzard can be deadly for people or animals caught outside.

7 Have you ever heard of "Tornado Alley?" "Tornado Alley" refers to an area in the middle of the United States, including South Dakota, Nebraska Kansas, Missouri, Oklahoma, Arkansas, Louisiana, and parts of North Dakota, Minnesota, Iowa, Ohio, Indiana, Illinois, Indiana, Kentucky, Tennessee and Texas. In this "alley," conditions are often right for a tornado, a violent and destructive windstorm, characterized by a funnel-shaped cloud that spins. Tornado winds can range in speed from around fifty to three hundred miles per hour and can literally lift objects thousands of feet into the air and drop them hundreds of miles away. One of the most dangerous things about tornadoes is they often form with little or no warning, making getting to safety more difficult than with hurricanes.

8 Weather can be very pleasant, like on lazy rainy days, or when there's just enough snow that school gets canceled. However, we should never forget that it can also be very extreme, and people's lives can be in danger. It is important to know what is going on with the weather in your area and, in extreme weather situations, to know what to do in order to stay safe. Don't ever underestimate how destructive the weather can be.

Questions

1. Which word or phrase DOES NOT mean almost the same thing as *statistics* in paragraph 4?
   a. facts and figures
   b. numbers
   c. good guesses
   d. calculations

2. What is a good definition of *participate* in paragraph 1?

____

3. What is the main theme of this article?
   a. there are lots of different kinds of weather
   b. it's important to keep in mind how deadly storms can be
   c. hurricanes and tornadoes have a lot in common
   d. the weather is usually pleasant

4. Explain the difference between a regular snowfall and a blizzard.

____

5. According to the map, which of these areas is in Tornado Alley?
   a. the eastern coastal portion
   b. the western coastal portion
   c. the central portion
   d. the northwest portion

Roger Staubach: Football Legend

1 There are many figures in sports history that stand out as remarkable, but few can compare to former Dallas Cowboys quarterback Roger Staubach. He was born on February 5, 1942 in Cincinnati, Ohio. After attending Catholic school, he enrolled in the United States Naval Academy. As a sophomore, Staubach became Navy's starting quarterback. In his junior year at the Naval Academy, he led the team to a #2 ranking, losing the Cotton Bowl to #1 ranked Texas. Navy also defeated Notre Dame, one of their fiercest rivals. That year Staubach won the Heisman Trophy, which is awarded to the best college football player in America

2 Staubach was a tenth round draft pick of the Dallas Cowboys in the 1964 National Football League (NFL) draft. However, he couldn't start playing professionally right away. As a graduate of the US Naval Academy, he was obligated to serve in the Navy for several years after graduation. Finally, in 1969, he arrived at the Dallas Cowboys training camp just in time to be able to play as a twenty-seven-year-old rookie.

3 Roger Staubach played football for the Dallas Cowboys from 1969 through 1979. In game eight of the 1971 season, he became the starting quarterback and led the team to ten consecutive wins, and to the Super Bowl. The Cowboys won the Super Bowl (the NFL championship) that year, and he was named Most Valuable Player (MVP).

4 Staubach was known for his patience as a quarterback, holding onto the football long enough to look for the perfect passing opportunity. One of most famous moments occurred during a 1975 playoff game against the Minnesota Vikings. The Cowboys were trailing 14 - 10 with only seconds left on the clock, when Staubach completed a fifty-yard bomb to one of his favorite wide receivers, Drew Pearson, who walked into the end zone for the winning touchdown. In a post-game interview, Staubach admitted he had prayed a "Hail Mary" right as he threw the pass. From then on in the NFL,

anytime a quarterback threw a last-ditch-effort pass, it was called a "Hail Mary" pass.

5 Staubach was known as "Roger the Dodger," because of his ability to scramble and avoid tackles. Another one of his nicknames was "Captain Comeback," due to his ability to turn the game around in the fourth quarter. During his career, he led the Cowboys to twenty-three game-winning drives in the fourth quarter, with seventeen of those being with less than two minutes left in the game or in overtime play.

6 Roger Staubach retired in 1979 with one of the most impressive records in football history. In regular game play, he had a fantastic seventy-five percent winning percentage. That means his team won three out of every four games they played, which is an incredibly high percentage. He was also a six-time Pro Bowl player and led the Cowboys to the Super Bowl four times. Staubach was inducted into the Pro Football Hall of Fame in 1985. He was also voted number twenty-nine on *The Sporting News* list top 100 football players in 1999. Roger Staubach is one of the few men who truly deserve to be called a football legend.

Questions

1. What does the word *sophomore* mean in paragraph 1? If you need to, use a dictionary to find the meaning.

    a. a person who goes to church every week
    b. a person who is over six feet tall
    c. a person who grew up in Ohio
    d. a person in the second year of college

2. What word or phrase would be a good synonym for *consecutive* in paragraph 3?

    a. total
    b. lucky
    c. in a row
    d. league championship

3. Divide consecutive into syllables.

____

4. What does MVP stand for?

____

5. Why did Roger Staubach miss out on several years of playing pro football?

____

6. What award did Staubach win for being the best college football player in the country?

____

7. What did Roger Staubach do after he retired from playing professional football?

a. he became a professional baseball player
b. he ran for President of the United States
c. he enrolled in the US Naval Academy
d. the article doesn't say

8. Do you think the author made a good argument that Roger Staubach is one of the greatest players in the history of professional football? Give reasons for your answer.

____

____

____

No Ordinary House Cats!

1 Did you know there are thirty-six different species of wild cats found all over the world? Wild cats are very intriguing animals. They are mammals - they're warm-blooded, have fur, give birth to live babies, and nurse their young. They are also quick and powerful, as well as being intelligent, skillful hunters.

2 One wild cat, the cheetah, is perhaps the most exotic of all the wild cats. It is a beautiful animal, yellowish in color with small dark spots. Its body, which is long, slender and muscular, resembles a greyhound's. The cheetah's long, thin legs are very powerful and make the animal nearly undefeatable in a chase. An adult cheetah can run up to 60 mph and can outrun any animal in a short distance quite easily. Also, the cheetah's paws are very dog-like, narrow with hard pads and short retractable claws. This makes the cheetah able to grip better when chasing its prey. The cheetah, unlike most cats, does not roar, but does purr and make other vocal sounds, from high-pitched barking to chirping sounds.

3 The cheetah is a magnificent hunter. It hunts mainly during the day and will follow herds of animals, looking for young, injured or older animals to prey upon. Due to the cheetah's great speed, it usually brings down the animal on the first try. Its large jaws allow the cheetah to grab the animal, normally around the windpipe, and hold it in its mouth until the animal suffocates.

4 Another very interesting wild cat is the puma, also known as the cougar, panther, or mountain lion. The size and color of the puma varies greatly

according to where it lives. In some areas, the puma has a longer coat, due to extremely cold temperatures, as in the higher mountainous regions. The cat's color also varies and can be slate grey, buff yellow, reddish brown and any variety in between. The puma has a small, broad head with small rounded ears. It has a powerful body, with long hind legs and a long tail, with black on its tip.

5 The puma prefers to hunt alone, either during the day or at night. Sometimes the puma will cache, or store its kill in densely covered brush and go back to it and feed over several days. The puma is big enough to be able to tackle large farm animals, such as a cow or a horse. This makes him very unpopular with ranchers and farmers. Pumas also prey upon deer, sheep, rodents, rabbits, and beavers. During the hunt, the puma uses its powerful hind legs to lunge at its prey with running jumps that can stretch as far as 40 feet.

6 Perhaps the most powerful cat is the jaguar. The jaguar is often confused with the leopard, because they are both yellowish/tan in color with dark markings (called rosettes). However, looking more closely at the jaguar, you notice it has small dots or shapes inside the rosette markings, unlike the leopard. The jaguar prefers to live in forest areas, close to water and lives mostly in the central and northern parts of South America. It is the biggest cat on the continent.

7 The jaguar has no real rivals. No other predator can compete with its power and size. When the jaguar goes hunting depends largely on where it lives. If it lives closer to human population, it usually hunts at night. It preys upon a range of many different animals and has such powerful jaws that it is able to pierce through its prey's skull with one swift bite.

8 Wild cats are truly remarkable creatures. Besides the cheetah, puma, and jaguar, there are dozens more, each one fascinating in its own way. Learning more about these beautiful creatures is a great way to spend some spare time.

Questions

1. Which word in paragraph one means *extremely interesting*?

____

2. Which word in paragraph 2 means *extremely unusual*?

____

3. Among cheetahs, pumas, and jaguars, which one is the fastest? Explain your answer.

____

4. Which of the three cats is considered strongest? Explain your answer.

____

5. Do pumas have rosettes?

Yes

No

6. Divide *intriguing* into syllables.

____

7. Divide *retractable* into syllables.

____

8. In paragraph 3, what does *suffocates* mean?

____

9. If a reader didn't know what *suffocates* mean, what clue would be helpful in figuring out the meaning?

____

10. Was this article written mainly to entertain, or mainly to inform?

____

Conventions of Standard English

Relative Pronouns and Adverbs

Relative Pronouns

Relative pronouns are words we use that introduce a dependent clause, which refers back to a noun or a pronoun and gives us more information about it.

Relative pronouns combine two thoughts to make our sentences sound much better and smoother. Read these two sentences:

Here is a book. It is a book with over 500 pages.

We can express the same thoughts in one sentence:

Here is a book that has over 500 pages.

That sentence says the same thing as the other two sentences, but with fewer words, which is almost always better than using a lot of words. The sentence uses the relative pronoun *that* to refer to the book, and to tie both thoughts together. The entire phrase *that has over 500 pages* is the dependent clause that tells us more about the book.

The most common relative pronouns are: *that, which, who, whom, whose.*

Whoever and *whichever* are two more relative pronouns you can use.

The word *that* can refer to people, places or things, but *which* should only be used when referring to places or things. The word *whose* can refer to people, places or things. The words *who* and *whom* always refer to people. These two can be tricky. Just remember to use *who* to refer to *they, we, he, she* or *I*, and whom to refer to *them, us, him, her* or *me*.

Relative Adverbs

Relative adverbs are a lot like relative pronouns. The difference is that they introduce a clause which modifies a verb, not a noun or a pronoun. Common relative adverbs include: *how, where, why, when, whenever* and *wherever*.

It's All Relative

In this exercise, fill in the blank with the correct relative pronoun or adverb.

1. _________ wants my old baseball glove can have it.

2. Do you remember _________ you put the mop bucket?

3. This is my classmate _________ I told you about.

4. I can't wait until the day _________ I turn 16.

5. My cousin Evan is the one _________ was on the quiz show.

6. The cat _________ gave birth to seven kittens last year is back.

7. _________ activity you choose is fine with me.

8. Can you show me _________ to tie a bowtie?

9. This is my friend Esmerelda, _________ mother was born in Mexico

10. The watch _________ my grandfather gave me is very old.

11. Minnesota, _________ my grandparents live, gets a lot of snow.

12. We went to the State Fair of Texas, _________ is the biggest state fair in America.

13. The author of the book *Pancake Puppies*, _________ is very funny, is coming to speak at our school.

14. What's important is not if you win or lose, but _________ you play the game.

15. Do you still have the book _________ you borrowed from the library?

Progressive Verb Tenses

Progressive Verb Tenses

Verb tenses are all about time. There's present tense:

I sleep eight hours every night.

There's past tense:

I slept eight hours last night.

Then there's future tense:

I will sleep eight hours tonight.

These are the verb tenses we use most often, but there are other ones that we use a lot, too. Let's look at progressive tenses.

Present progressive tense: this is used when a verb describes an action that is continuous, and is going on right now:

The teacher is grading the tests.

Past progressive tense: this tense is used when you're talking about something that was happening in the past. Often it's used to describe something that was happening when something else happened.

The teacher was grading the tests last night.
The teacher was grading the tests when the fire alarm went off.

Future progressive tense: this tense is used for an action that will happen in the future and is an ongoing action.

The teacher will be grading the tests while the students are at gym class.
I will be doing my homework after school.

Progressive Tense Exercises

Rewrite these five sentences in present progressive tense.

1. I watch TV.

____

2. I ride my bike.

____

3. I wash my hair.

____

4. I eat lunch.

____

5. I play chess.

____

Rewrite these five sentence pairs. Combine them into one sentence using the past progressive tense.

Example: We had lots of fun. Then it started raining.
We were having lots of fun until it started raining.

6. We slept. The thunderstorm started.

____

7. We studied for the test. We didn't want to fail.

____

8. We swam in the deep end of the pool. The lifeguard announced the pool was closing.

____

9. We read quietly. The teacher announced a surprise quiz.

____

10. I watched videos on my phone. Then the battery died.

____

In these five sentences, fill in the blank spaces with the future progressive tense of the verb shown in parentheses.

11. Which teams (play) _________ _________ _________ for the championship?

12. I (study) _________ _________ _________ _________ _________ all night long.

13. I (watch) _________ _________ _________ the mailbox for your letter.

14. We (travel) _________ _________ _________ to Europe this summer.

15. My cousins (arrive) _________ _________ _________ _________ _________ any minute now.

Modal Verbs

Modal Verbs

Some verbs are known as helping verbs. They are called that because they always come along with a main verb, and help give the main verb more precise meaning. There are different kinds of helping verbs, including **modal verbs**. The modal verbs are: *ought to, will, should, might, shall, may, must, could, would, can*. Modal verbs are used to express several different things, such as ability, likelihood, permission, advice, habits, obligation, requests, availability, possibility, necessity, certainty, etc. Modal verbs can be used in both statements, and questions.

Here is an example of a modal verb expressing *ability*:

Jamal can get straight A's without even trying.

In that sentence, *get* is the main verb, and *can* is the modal verb. The speaker is saying that Jamal has the ability to get straight A's quite easily.

Here's a modal verb expressing *permission*:

You kids may have one cookie apiece.

Here's one expressing *likelihood*, or *probability*:

John might be late for the meeting.

Here is one that expresses *advice*:

You should not spend so much time watching TV.

Here is a modal verb in question form:

Mom, may I go to the parade with Grandma and Grandpa?

Modal Verbs Exercise

Look at the word in front of each sentence. Fill in the blank space in each sentence with a modal verb to express that thought.

ability, likelihood, permission, advice, habits, obligation, requests, availability, possibility, necessity, certainty

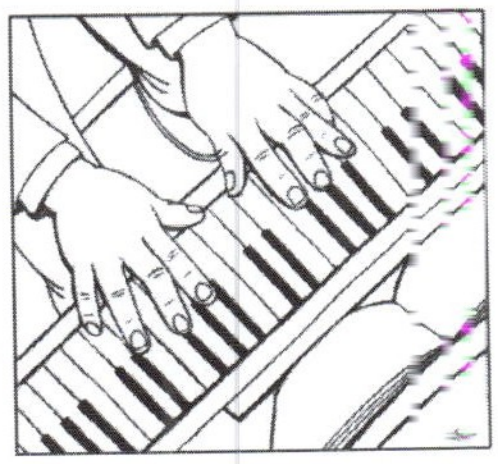

1. ABILITY: Our music teacher says Mark ______ play the piano better than anyone else in my class.

2. LIKELIHOOD: Shirley said she ______ be able to come over after school, but the decision will be up to her mom.

3. PERMISSION: Dad, ______ I stay up late to watch the end of the ballgame?

4. ADVICE: You ______ study harder to make sure you pass the test.

5. HABITS: When you were a baby, you ______ play with your rattle for hours at a time.

6. OBLIGATION: Sally, you simply ______ start cleaning out the litter box every day!

7. LIKELIHOOD: The students have been working on the project all day so they ______ be almost finished.

8. AVAILABILITY: ______ you repair it this afternoon?

9. CERTAINTY: That clock ______ be right; there's no way it's bedtime already.

10. ABILITY: I'm so hungry I ______ eat a horse!

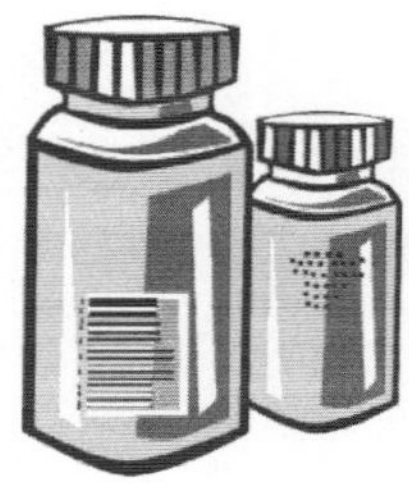

11. OBLIGATION: You ______ take your medicine every morning before school.

12. CERTAINTY: Doug has never missed a day of school before, so he ______ be really sick.

13. ABILITY: If I were just two inches taller, I ______ reach the top shelf.

14. OBLIGATION: We ______ ______ thank Mom for all her hard work on the meal.

15. CERTAINTY: Tom is usually eager to help, so I predict he _____ be the first one to volunteer.

Adjective Order

Adjective Order

Adjectives modify nouns or noun phrases. They describe things. For example:

The **red** vase
The **cute** puppy
The **buttermilk** pancakes

The highlighted words in the phrases above are adjectives. They give us more information about the vase, the puppy, and the pancakes. However, there are many more things that could be said about each of these things. It's fine to use more than one adjective to describe something. Look at these:

The **old red** vase
The **cute little brown** puppy
The **delicious homemade buttermilk** pancakes

Again, the words in bold are adjectives. Now we know even more about the vase, the puppy and the pancakes, because we have more than one adjective describing each thing. However, when we use more than one adjective in front of a noun or noun phrase, we must make sure to use them in the right order, or our phrase will sound awkward and unnatural. Let's rearrange the adjectives in the above passages:

The **red old** vase
The **brown little cute** puppy
The **buttermilk homemade delicious** pancakes.

See how awkward these passages sound now? That's because the adjectives are out of order. When using more than one adjective, we must put them in the following order:

Opinion (this is *your* opinion of something) - cute, smart, beautiful, expensive, delicious, tasty, boring, exciting, handsome, brilliant, etc.

Size - small, big, huge, tiny, large, tall, short, little, etc.

Shape - round, square, oval, rectangular, triangular, bumpy, flat, etc.

Age - young, old, elderly, antique, teenage, modern, ancient, new, etc.

Color - red, blue, plaid, yellow, orange, green, brown, etc.

Origin - American, Canadian, foreign, French, Mexican, Pacific, homemade, etc.

Material - wooden, buttermilk, steel, wool, plastic, brick, pepperoni, rubber, etc.

Keep in mind that sometimes you'll run into an exception to this rule, and following this order will result in a passage that sounds awkward. When that happens, use the adjective order that sounds the most natural. Also, you should rarely (if ever) use more than three adjectives in a row, unless you're doing it deliberately to be humorous, or you're writing informally to someone you know well. That's because using more than three adjectives in a row almost always sounds awkward, even if they're in the correct order.

Adjective Order Exercise

Read each passage, and then choose the correct order of adjectives from the choices below the passage. If you think the passage already has the adjectives in the correct order, choose NO CHANGE.

1. the yellow old big bus
   a. NO CHANGE
   b. the old yellow big bus
   c. the big yellow old bus
   d. the big old yellow bus

2. the small round frying pan
   a. NO CHANGE
   b. the round small frying pan
   c. the frying small round pan
   d. the small frying round pan

3. the French tall young player
   a. NO CHANGE
   b. the tall young French player
   c. the young French tall player
   d. the young tall French player

4. the Canadian old hilarious clown
   a. NO CHANGE
   b. the Canadian hilarious old clown
   c. the hilarious old Canadian clown
   d. the old Canadian hilarious clown

5. the brown huge wooden spoon
   a. NO CHANGE
   b. the wooden brown huge spoon
   c. the wooden huge brown spoon
   d. the huge brown wooden spoon

6. the new exciting foreign novel
    a. NO CHANGE
    b. the foreign exciting new novel
    c. the exciting new foreign novel
    d. the new foreign exciting novel

7. the ugly two-story old mansion
    a. NO CHANGE
    b. the old ugly two-story mansion
    c. the ugly old two-story mansion
    d. the two-story old ugly mansion

8. the modest new boxing champion
    a. NO CHANGE
    b. the new modest boxing champion
    c. the boxing new modest champion
    d. the modest boxing new champion

9. the teenage heroic Mexican lifeguard
    a. NO CHANGE
    b. the heroic teenage Mexican lifeguard
    c. the teenage Mexican heroic lifeguard
    d. the Mexican teenage heroic lifeguard

10. the huge rectangular pepperoni pizza
    a. NO CHANGE
    b. the rectangular pepperoni huge pizza
    c. the pepperoni huge rectangular pizza
    d. the huge pepperoni rectangular pizza

Prepositions and Prepositional Phrases

Preposition

The **preposition** is an important part of speech. Prepositions are words that are come before nouns or pronouns, and tell us something about the noun or pronoun, such as location, time, or how it relates to something else. They get their name from the fact that they come before ("pre-position") nouns and pronouns. This does not mean that there aren't any words between the preposition and the noun or pronoun; in fact, usually there is at least one word between them (but not always). It just means that the preposition never comes after the noun or pronoun it's referring to. There are well over a hundred prepositions in English. Here are some of the most common ones:

about above across after against along among around at before behind below beneath beside between beyond by down during except for from in inside into like near of off on out over past regarding since through to toward under underneath until up upon with within without

Here are some examples:
The boy **in** the uniform is named Bobby.
I put the pencil **on** my desk.
This book is **about** soccer.
I tripped **over** the log.
I sat quietly **during** church.

Preposition Exercise

In each sentence, circle the preposition.

1. My parents got married in that church.

2. Do you know if Pedro went to summer camp?

3. Kids, I want you home by lunchtime!

4. I like the ring in that window.

5. What do you think we should do regarding the missing cupcake?

6. May I please have another helping of potato salad?

7. You should always vacuum under the rug.

8. Draw a circle around each noun.

9. The player on second base hit a grand slam last inning.

10. I was the first one who went down the slide.

Prepositional Phrases

A **prepositional phrase** is a group of words, or phrase, that modifies another word, or group of words. Prepositional phrases make up a large portion of our spoken and written language, and it's important to understand how to interpret them, and how to make them. All prepositional phrases begin with a preposition, and have an object. Here are some examples:

We rode our bikes ***for an hour.***
This tells us how long they rode their bikes.

After breakfast*, we went* ***to church****.*
This tells us when they went (after breakfast), and where they went (to church).

The kitten was scared, so she hid ***under the couch****.*
This tells us where the kitten hid.

We should be there ***before dark****.*
This tells us when they should get to their destination.

The stain ***on the counter*** *finally came out* ***after I scrubbed and scrubbed****.*
This tells us where the stain was, and when it came out.

All the words in bold in the sentences above are prepositional phrases. A prepositional phrase needs at least two things: a preposition, and an object of the preposition. Let's illustrate this from the sentences above - on the left side of the divider is the preposition; on the right side is the object:

for / an hour   *After / breakfast*   *to / church*   *under / the couch*

before / dark   *on / the counter*   *after / I scrubbed and scrubbed*

Also, as you can see from the above sentences, a prepositional phrase can be an adjective phrase that modifies a noun or pronoun, or it can be an adverb phrase that modifies a verb.

Find the Prepositional Phrase

In each sentence, circle the prepositional phrase. Then decide if the prepositional phrase is functioning as an adjective, or as an adverb. Write ADJ at the end of the sentence if it's an adjective phrase; write ADV at the end of the sentence if it's an adverb phrase.

1. Look before you leap.

2. Don't rush into things.

3. Many people across the nation support the proposal.

4. A stitch in time saves nine.

5. An ounce of prevention is very expensive nowadays.

6. Let's play volleyball after lunch.

7. Class, do not speak during the test period.

8. I'm torn between two opinions.

9. Except for Lawanda, the entire class failed the spelling test.

10. Fluffy, get off the couch this instant!

Complete Sentences, Sentence Fragments, and Run-on Sentences

Complete Sentences

Sentences are the way we express our thoughts in speaking or writing. Very few words (such as *stop* | *hurry* | *yes* | *come* | *hello* | *goodbye*) can express a complete thought without being combined with other words. Except for these extremely rare exceptions, it takes more than one word to express a complete thought. A group of words that expresses a complete thought, followed by a period, question mark, or exclamation point is a sentence, or a **complete sentence**. In order to express a complete thought, a sentence must have two things - a **subject**, and a **predicate**. The subject is the person place or thing the sentence is about. The predicate tells the reader or listener something about the subject. A predicate always contains a verb. Here are some examples of complete sentences, with the predicate in bold:

The teacher ***greeted his students****.*

It ***rains a lot in Seattle****.*

Football ***is my favorite sport.***

Did *you* ***enjoy the book****?*

Dogs ***bark****.*

In some sentences, the subject isn't actually shown. These are called imperative sentences, because they give an order, or a command. The subject in this kind of sentence is always *you* (the person or thing the command or order is being given to), even though *you* doesn't appear in the sentence. There is a special name for the subject in an imperative sentence - it is called *the understood you.* Here are some examples of sentences which have *the understood you* as the subject; each of these is actually a complete sentence:

Stop!
Read quietly until recess.
Sit up and beg for a doggy biscuit!
Get over here as soon as possible.
Don't do that.

Complete Sentence Exercise

In each sentence below, draw a circle around the predicate.

1. Stop right there.

2. Caitlin gave her grandmother a hug.

3. I enjoyed reading that book.

4. Susan and Rhonda are coming over tonight.

5. I think that's incorrect.

6. Mom ran a 10k.

7. My sister is 14 years old.

8. Our planet revolves around the sun.

9. Your new bike is awesome.

10. John is taller than Jim.

Sentence Fragments

What if you have a bunch of words, and a period, question mark, or exclamation point, but either the subject or verb is missing? In that case, you don't have a complete sentence; you have a **sentence fragment**. When we're speaking to a friend or family member, we use sentence fragments all the time, and that's OK, because that kind of speech is extremely informal, and no one expects us to follow all the rules of grammar. However, sentence fragments are unacceptable in writing, because when we write something, we can take the time to make sure we're using proper grammar. Here are some sentence fragments:

Our bikes.
Behind the TV.
As soon as you can.
Since we got up so late.
Although we did our best.

The first two fragments have no verb, which makes it easy to understand why they're fragments. However, the last three contain both a subject and verb. So why are they fragments? They're fragments because each one contains a subordinating conjunction, which means the phrase is a dependent clause. Dependent clauses can never stand alone; they always depend on a main clause.

Fragment or Complete Sentence Exercise

Read each group of words below. If it's a complete sentence, write C in the blank space. If it's a sentence fragment, write F in the blank space.

1. Because I said so. _____

2. Is this what you ordered? _____

3. Since you already told Sally. _____

4. Whenever you're ready. ____

5. Hurry up! ____

6. I can't stand pea soup. ____

7. Everyone in my class. ____

8. Until it's time to go to bed. ____

9. That's hilarious! ____

10. Where's my math book? ____

Run-on Sentences

Using **run-on sentences** is another common error in English. A run-on sentence is a sentence that's made up of two or more complete sentences, with either no punctuation separating them, or the wrong punctuation separating them. Here are some examples:

It's been raining all day the river is about to flood.

This road is very dangerous you should reduce your speed.

The teacher said there would be a quiz on Friday and this made Jenny very anxious because she had been very busy taking care of her sick mother all week and she hadn't had time to read the textbook or do her homework and she began to worry that she would fail the test.

Let's look at these sentences and see why they're run-on sentences.

It's been raining all day the river is about to flood.

This is two complete sentences with no punctuation between them. It should be rewritten with a semi-colon between *day* and *the*, or a comma and a word like so or and between them, or it should be turned into two separate sentences, separated by a period.

It's been raining all day; the river is about to flood.

It's been raining all day, so the river is about to flood.

It's been raining all day. The river is about to flood.

The next sentence is similar:

This road is very dangerous, you should reduce your speed.

This could be turned into two separate sentences separated by a period, but it would sound abrupt and awkward. It would be better to use a semi-colon between *dangerous* and *should*, or add the word *so* after the comma: *This road is very dangerous; you should reduce your speed.*

This road is very dangerous, so you should reduce your speed.

The next sentence is simply too long and complicated; the writer is trying to cram too much information into one sentence. It should be divided up into more than one sentence, by removing *because* and *and*, and adding some periods:

The teacher said there would be a quiz on Friday and this worried Jenny. She had been very busy taking care of her sick mother all week and she hadn't had time to read the textbook or do her homework. She feared that she would fail the test.

Run-on Sentence Exercise

Read each sentence below. If it's a complete sentence, write C in the blank space. If it's a run-on sentence, write R in the blank space.

1. That's easy for you to say you don't even need to study to pass. _____

2. Billy is in fourth grade and he likes pancakes and he likes football and he speaks Spanish. _____

3. If you're going to be late, please call ahead to let us know. _____

4. It's starting to rain; we should go inside. _____

5. Soccer is boring, and I don't like playing it or watching it. _____

6. It's getting late we should head home. _____

7. What time is it? _____

8. Mom said I have to clean the garage, you should help me. _____

9. Don't just stand there; do something. _____

10. I wish I had a nickel for every book I've read I'd be a rich man. _____

Frequently Confused Words

Homophones are words that sound alike, but are spelled differently, and have different meanings. It's easy to make a mistake and use the wrong word when writing, so it's important to make sure you choose the correct word. Here are some examples of homophones which are commonly misused:

to, two, too | there, their, they're | for, four| its it's | male, mail | your, you're | right, write

flower, flour | know, no | son, sun | steal, steel | pear, pair | hole, whole | peace | piece | heal, heel

wait, weight | waste, waist | toe, tow | stair, stare | wear, where | bear, bare | buy, by | dear, deer

break, brake | pour, poor | hour, our | knot, not | hear, here | plain, plane | principal, principle

Those are some of the most frequently misused words, but there are many others which you'll run into from time to time. Unfortunately, there are no easy rules you can memorize to help you use the right word every time. You simply have to memorize the different spellings and meanings, and practice using them a lot, so it becomes a habit to use the word with the correct meaning. Here are some exercises to help you.

Homophone Exercise

For each sentence, circle the word on the right that belongs in the blank space

1. I received a ribbon from the ________ for perfect attendance.	principal	principle	
2. We need more ________ for the cake recipe.	flower	flour	
3. My sister turned ________ years old yesterday.	four	for	
4. You can come, ________.	to	two	too
5. You read the ________ book already?	whole	hole	
6. This is expensive, so don't ________ it.	waste	waist	
7. Say, ________ about time for football season to start.	it's	its	
8. Leave the kitten with ________ mother for now.	it's	its	
9. Take these apples ________ Mrs. Gonzalez.	two	to	too
10. I think your coat is over ________.	their	they're	there
11. I hope I got the answer ________ .	write	right	
12. Eating a lot of fast food will make you gain ________.	weight	wait	
13. The sink is made of stainless ________.	steal	steel	

14. Where did your cousins say ________ from?	they're their there
15. A bicycle has ________ wheels, but a unicycle has only one.	too to two
16. It is impolite to ________ at people.	stare stair
17. There's only one ________ of birthday cake left.	peace piece
18. You should never approach a ________ because they're dangerous.	bear bare
19. You press on the ________ lever when you want to stop.	break brake
20. My aunt and uncle have one ________ and two daughters.	sun son
21. There are exactly sixty minutes in one ________.	hour our
22. They are running late because ________ car had a flat tire.	they're their there
23. Please ________ your grandmother another glass of iced tea.	pour poor
24. I need you to pick me up some ________ manila envelopes.	plane plain
25. I think this old ________ of shoes is just about worn out.	pear pair

Capitalization

Proper **capitalization** is very important in writing. Improper capitalization can cause a reader to think the writer isn't very smart. Many people won't pay any attention to writing that contains capitalization errors. In high school and college, making capitalization mistakes on the papers you will need to write may result in a failing grade. So it's vital that you learn how to use proper capitalization. Fortunately, the main rules are easy to learn and follow. Here they are:

Titles (books, movies, songs, etc.): The first and last word of the title should always be capitalized. All other words should also be capitalized, except for *a, an, the, and, or, nor,* and all prepositions shorter than four letters (*in, by, to, at, of, off, on*, etc.). These words should be lower case, unless they are the first or last word of the title. *The Dawn of Time, The Muppets Take Manhattan, Raiders of the Lost Ark*

Proper nouns: names of people, businesses, pets, cities, states, buildings, monuments, continents, rivers, oceans, countries, celestial objects and areas, landmarks, organizations, departments, government agencies, etc., should all be capitalized. *Mrs. Smith, Jose Ramirez, Fluffy, Dallas, France, New York, Jupiter, Washington Monument, Internal Revenue Service, United Airlines, Department of Engineering Technology, Sinclair Community College, Eastside Junior High School, the Red Sea, the Milky Way, Empire State Building, the Great Pyramid*

Titles (of people): these should be capitalized when used with the person's name - *Doctor Jones, Coach Brown, Mayor Crutcher, Judge Thompson*, etc. However, they should not be capitalized on their own – *the doctor is in, the judge gave him a stern lecture, our mayor will be giving a speech, the coach led the team to victory*, etc.

Salutations and closings in correspondence: Always capitalize the first word of your salutation (greeting) and first word of closing when writing to someone: *Dear Aunt Mary, Esteemed colleagues, Sincerely yours,* etc.

Words derived from proper nouns: *Mexican, New Yorker, Texan, Germanic, Martian, English, Worcestershire sauce, Canadian bacon*

Geographical areas: *New England, Silicon Valley, the Pacific Northwest, the Midwest, the Upper Peninsula*

Important historical events or eras: *the Civil War, the Protestant Reformation, the California Gold Rush, the Middle Ages, the Enlightenment, the Bolshevik Revolution*

Days of the week, months, holidays: *January, Thanksgiving, Christmas, Monday, New Year's Eve, Tuesday, July, Yom Kippur*

Religions, holy books, and deities: *God, Allah, Jesus, Jehovah, Krishna, the Bible, the Torah, the Koran, the New Testament*

When quoting someone, capitalize the first word of the quote: *Mom said, "Your teacher told us you're making great progress."* .

Those are the main capitalization rules that you need to know. There are a few other minor rules, but you won't need to know them for a while, and even then, you'll rarely have a need to use them. The main rules above aren't hard to learn at all, and you probably already follow a lot of the rules without even knowing they're rules.

Capitalization Exercise

Read each numbered item, and then decide if it's capitalized correctly, or incorrectly. If it's capitalized correctly, write NO CHANGE in the blank space below the item. If it's capitalized incorrectly, rewrite it in the blank space, using proper capitalization.

1. (title) Five Things You Should Know About Rattlesnakes

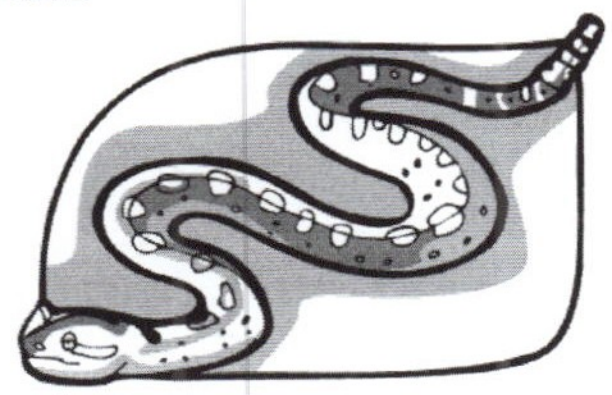

____

2. (title) that's easy for you to say!

____

3. (title) cheaper by the Dozen

____

4. Chicago, illinois

____

5. I would like to make an appointment with doctor Jones.

____

6. "be careful, Frank!" yelled coach Johnson.

____

7. After the Game, a Reporter interviewed the Coach.

____

8. Last year on vacation, we went to yellowstone national park.

____

9. Dr. Bramley is Chairman of the Department of Astronomy.

____

10. Muslims believe in allah and follow the teachings of the koran.

____

11. Bill Gates was the founder of the company called microsoft.

____

12. My great-grandfather fought in world war II.

____

13. Christmas and new year's day are always one week apart.

____

14. (letter salutation) dear reverend Swanson,

____

15. In my opinion, no salad is complete without italian dressing.

____

Commas and Quotation Marks

Commas and **quotation marks** must both be used in dialogue. A dialogue is simply when two or more people are talking. Also, when writing about what a person is thinking, but not saying out loud, follow the very same rules.

Look at these sentences:

"Look, students," Mrs. Jefferson exclaimed, "there's a hummingbird!"

Mike said, "I owe you a huge favor, Mandy."

The commas and quotation marks help readers understand what is being said, as well as who is saying it, and they help keep readers from getting confused. Always remember that you can never have only one quotation mark by itself. Quotation marks must always come in pairs – one at the beginning of the dialogue being quoted, and one at the end. The final quotation mark should come after the comma, period, question mark or exclamation point.

Commas and periods always go before the final quotation mark, but when a sentence starts with a quotation that ends in a question mark or an exclamation point, you should *not* use a comma:

"And just where do you think you're going?" the detective demanded to know.

"We're the new league champions!" Marcus shouted.

Commas and Quotation Marks Exercise

Each of these sentences is either missing one or more commas and one or more sets of quotation marks, or both. Rewrite each sentence with the missing commas and quotation marks on the blank line below it.

1. Do you know what time it is the little girl asked.

____

2. That's strange thought Cindy the puppy was just here but now he's gone.

____

3. Mrs. Rojas said Please raise your hand if you're still working on the test.

____

4. Mom asked Who wants to help me with the dishes?

____

5. Bonnie said I think that's the best field trip we've ever been on.

____

Commas in Coordinating Conjunctions and Compound Sentences

A **coordinating conjunction** is a word that connects words, phrases, or clauses. They're easy to remember, because there are only seven of them: *for, and, nor, but, or, yet, so*. You can use the acronym FANBOYS to help you remember them all. While you should be familiar with all seven of them, you'll actually only use or encounter four of them on a regular basis: *and, but, or, so*. You'll see and use these four several times during a typical day. Every now and then you'll use or encounter *nor* or *yet*, but you'll rarely run into or use *for* as a coordinating conjunction these days.

A sentence that contains two independent clauses is called a compound sentence. An independent clause is a group of words that express a complete thought, and could be a complete sentence all by itself. Compound sentences are made up of two independent clauses joined together by a coordinating conjunction, and they always need a comma before the coordinating conjunction. The only exception is if the sentence is very short.

Coordinating Conjunctions Exercise

Turn each pair of sentences into one compound sentence, by using a coordinating conjunction and a comma.

1. I'm a light sleeper. My sister is a very deep sleeper.

____

2. I play soccer. I am becoming a better player every year.

____

3. Do you want to play checkers? Do you want to play chess?

____

4. It was raining very hard. I grabbed my umbrella.

____

5. We went to the zoo. We went to the art museum.

____

Spelling

Spelling Exercise

Read each definition, and then choose the answer with the correctly spelled word

1. a large sailboat

    a. yot
    b. yaht
    c. yacht
    d. yat

2. flimsy or easily damaged
    a. fragile
    b. frajile
    c. fraggil
    d. fragile

3. happening often
    a. frequent
    b. freaquent
    c. freequent
    d. frequint

4. used for keeping food and drinks cold
    a. reefrijerator
    b. refrigerator
    c. refrijerater
    d. refridgerator

5. make someone mad
   a. anoy
   b. annouy
   c. anouy
   d. annoy

6. having to do with the sun
   a. soler
   b. soaler
   c. solir
   d. solar

7. the inside part
   a. inferior
   b. interior
   c. inteereor
   d. intearior

8. worthy of trust
   a. onnest
   b. honest
   c. honnest
   d. onnust

9. to be unsure about
   a. doubt
   b. dout
   c. dought
   d. dowt

10. earlier
   a. preeviusly
   b. previously
   c. preeviously
   d. previusly

Knowledge of Language

Choosing Words and Phrases to Communicate Ideas Precisely

When speaking or writing, it's important to make our meaning as clear as we can. After all, the very purpose of writing or speaking is to communicate a specific message to someone else. Some ways of getting a message across are more effective than others. You can usually choose from several different ways of saying something, but in most cases, some of them will be much better choices than others.

Being Concise

The first general rule to keep in mind is that it's usually not a good idea to use a lot of words when a few would do. Using as few words as possible helps make the idea that you're trying to express stand out more clearly, instead of getting lost in a jumble of words. Using as few words as necessary is called being **concise**.

Compare these two ways a football player might talk to his teammates during practice:

It's important that every one of us on the team tries to do our very best to play as well as we can in order for us to be able to win the next game on the schedule.

We all need to do our best to win the next game.

The second sentence expresses the very same message as the first one, but does so much more effectively. There are times when it's necessary to use a lot of words, but when it's not necessary, it's usually much more effective to use only a few.

Being Concise Exercise

Read each sentence or phrase, and then rewrite it to say the same thing with fewer words.

1. I arrive at school every weekday, Monday through Friday, at 8 AM in the morning.

____

2. During the period of time when the California Gold Rush was taking place

____

3. Joe was smiling on account of the fact that he passed the test.

____

4. In the event that it starts raining all of a sudden, we'll go inside.

____

5. At the present time in history, there are 50 states in America.

____

Denotation and Connotation

There are many words that have very similar dictionary definitions, but have very different effects on the listener or reader. For example, both *slender* and *scrawny* mean *thin*, but *slender* is almost always considered to be a compliment, while *scrawny* would usually be taken as an insult. If someone who talks a lot is a friend of ours, we might describe him as *talkative*, but someone who doesn't like him would probably say he's just a *loudmouth*.

The dictionary definition of a word is called the **denotation**; the feeling it causes in a reader or listener is called the **connotation**. Words which have similar denotations, such as *scrawny* and *slender*, are called **synonyms**. Two synonyms can share the same connotation (such as *brave* and *courageous*), but in many cases synonyms have different connotations (such as *big* and *enormous*).

Knowing the different connotations of synonyms and using them accurately is a big part of communicating ideas precisely. Many times you'll be able to do so naturally, without even having to think about it, but there will be many other occasions when you'll want to take the time to choose the exact word that's most appropriate.

Denotation and Connotation Exercise

1. The word *miserly* has a negative connotation. Which word has a similar meaning to *miserly*, but with a positive connotation?
    - a. cheap
    - b. thrifty
    - c. greedy
    - d. penny-pinching

2. Which of these synonyms for *fat* would you use to describe a friend's cute 1 year-old brother?

a. obese
b. enormous
c. burly
d. plump

3. Which word is usually a negative synonym for *helper*?

a. accomplice
b. aide
c. assistant
d. partner

4. Which word would let a reader know that something is extremely *cold*?

a. cool
b. frosty
c. chilly
d. frigid

5. Which person below is the most *scared*?

a. a worried parent
b. an anxious investor
c. a terrified camper
d. a frightened neighbor

6. Which of these synonyms for *said* would most likely be used by one cashier telling another about a customer who was very angry?

a. whispered
b. asserted
c. announced
d. snarled

7. Each of these phrases has a meaning similar to *wrong conduct*. Which has the most negative connotation?

a. wicked behavior
b. improper actions
c. unsuitable acts
d. inappropriate deeds

8. You're pretty sure Shelley is mad at you because you saw her _________ at you.

a. looking
b. glaring
c. staring
d. glancing

9. Which person is experiencing the most sadness?

a. someone who is disappointed
b. someone who is unhappy
c. someone who is devastated
d. someone who is disheartened

10. Which of these actions would move you the farthest?

a. hop
b. jump
c. leap
d. skip

Use Punctuation to Create the Right Effect

Just as we can decide what effect to have on a reader by choosing which words to use in certain situations, we can also use punctuation to bring about different effects. The two punctuation marks that are best known for this are the question mark and the exclamation point. However, they are not the only ones we can use. We can use dashes, colons and semicolons for this purpose, too. You've seen these many times in your reading. Here's what they look like:

dash –
colon :
semicolon ;

So, how do we use dashes, colons, and semicolons for effect? Dashes are great when we want to bring attention to something by restating it in other words, giving more details about it, identify it, or stress it by repeating it.

It was three years ago that the greatest pet a person could ever ask for–Sir Barkalot–showed up on my doorstep.

That's the biggest pumpkin I've seen this Halloween–or any Halloween.

Billy, I've asked you three times now–three times–to take out the trash.
I make time for my fun activities–video games, comic books, soccer–only after I've finished my homework.

They can also be used with an **appositive**. An appositive is a word (or group of words) that renames or tells the reader more about another word (or group of words):

My mom's chili–which has secret ingredients I can't reveal–is the best chili in the world.

Dashes also come in handy for suddenly adding a thought, or changing tone:

I can't imagine where Fluffy could be hiding—wait, she's probably under the couch.

Corey is the best athlete in 4th grade - and the worst speller.

Colons have a lot in common with dashes, but aren't quite as strong. When a colon appears, it tells the reader that the rest of the sentence will sum up or explain what came before. However, the effect isn't quite as strong as the effect that comes from using a dash:

My cat has only one flaw: she's so cute I want to stay home from school and pet her all day.

I knew instantly who had eaten the last cookie: my little brother Garth.

Semicolons are used to show that there is some sort of relationship between two independent clauses. Each clause could be a sentence of its own, but with a semicolon you can combine them to form one sentence to show the reader how closely related they are:

I worked hard on this report; I hope the teacher gives me a good grade.

Using semicolons also helps you avoid writing a bunch of short, choppy sentences all in a row. Keep in mind, however, that a semicolon can only join two independent clauses that are closely related. This is not a proper use of a semicolon, for example:

James is two inches taller than me; he goes to the Baptist church.

Those are two independent clauses, but they are not related to each other, because the fact that James is taller has nothing to do with where he goes to church. Therefore the sentence should be two separate sentences.

Using Punctuation for Effect Exercise

A. Correct each sentence by inserting *dashes* in the proper places.

1. The three Rs reading, ‘riting, and ‘rithmetic form the foundation of education.

2. The big game the one I've been telling you about all week starts in exactly one hour.

3. As the crowd cheered him on, Rico bent his knees, swung for the fences and struck out.

4. I can't believe I got a 100 on my math test a 100!

5. That's the first 100 I've ever gotten on a math test actually it's the first 100 I've ever gotten on any test.

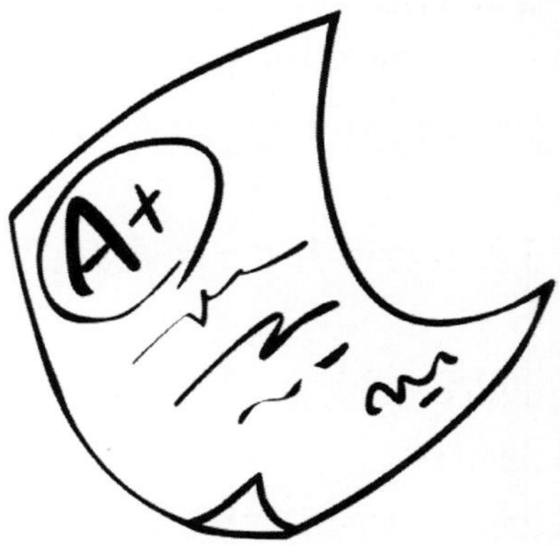

6. My favorite author the only one whose books I read again and again is J.K. Rowling.

B. Correct each sentence by inserting a *colon* in the proper place.

7. Four teams are left Chicago, Dallas, New York, and Los Angeles.

8. There's only one person who can save us Superman.

9. I only ask for one thing, class that everyone does his or her best.

10. I had to make a decision go to Ann's house after school, or go to Brenda's house.

C. Correct each sentence by inserting a *semicolon* in the proper place.

11. They lost again today that makes 20 games lost in a row.

12. It's half past five Grandma and Grandpa should be here any minute.

13. It looks like rain I'd better take an umbrella.

14. This is Tony's classroom Tammy's classroom is down the hall.

15. We have to arrive at school early we're going on a field trip.

Formal and Informal English

When we're talking to our friends and classmates, or writing an email to a pen pal, we don't use the same kind of language we would use if we were talking to the principal or writing a letter to a government official. We use informal language for people we know very well and are on our same level, but we use formal language when writing letters to people we don't know, or talking to adults about an important matter, etc. Here's an example of each:

Hi Wendy! I heard you're coming to town next week! I can't wait to see you!

Dear Ms. Jones, I have recently been informed that you will be arriving in town next week. I am eager to make your acquaintance.

There is a time and place for both kinds of language. When we use the wrong kind of language for the situation, however, it's inappropriate. If we used formal language around our friends on the playground, or to a classmate in an email, they would laugh at us. If we used informal language in the wrong situation, the reader or listener would be offended. Fortunately, it's usually pretty easy to tell which kind of English we should be using in a situation.

Formal and Informal English Exercise

In each numbered item, there is either a situation described, which calls for either formal or informal language, or there is an actual sentence or phrase, which is in either formal or informal language. In the blank space after each item, write F if the situation or language is formal; write I if the situation or language is informal.

1. You're writing a letter to your friend's parents to thank them for inviting you to your friend's birthday party. _____

2."Six bucks for a hot dog? These ballpark prices are crazy!" _____

3. "Please go ahead, sir. I believe you arrived before I did." _____

4. You're speaking at a city council meeting, asking the council to vote to build more parks and playgrounds. _____

5. You're describing a car accident you witnessed to a police officer. _____

6. "Hey, man, what's up?" _____

7. You're writing a note for your little brother. _____

8. You're writing a letter to the editor of the local newspaper about an upcoming election. _____

9. You're telling your best friend about your trip to a famous amusement park. _____

10. "That sounds awesome!" _____

Vocabulary Acquisition and Use

Vocabulary Exercise 1

Read each description, and then fill in the blank space with the word in the box that matches the description.

auditorium	seldom	accomplish	agriculture
suggest	mature	vertical	population
fortunate	compassion	curiosity	recognize
pleasure	admire	lecture	assist
slender	superb	pupil	massive

1. a student (or dark circle at center of eye)

____

2. raising crops or livestock for food

____

3. lucky, successful, blessed

____

4. big room or building where audiences gather to listen to speakers, singers, etc.

____

5. all the people who live in a certain place

____

6. to help; lend a hand to

____

7. up and down, not across

____

8. a speech or talk that informs or educates

____

9. to know who someone or something is from previous knowledge

____

10. to perform, complete, achieve, etc.

____

11. a strong desire to learn

____

12. to ask others to consider something; to recommend

____

13. slim, thin

____

14. fully grown

____

15. excellent, wonderful

____

16. not very often; rarely

____

17. feeling good; enjoyment

____

18. concern for others

____

19. very, very big

____

20. to respect or be fond of

____

Vocabulary Exercise 2

Read each description, and then fill in the blank space with the word in the box that matches the description.

decrease	thrifty	biology	foreign
annually	coarse	boundary	circular
request	environment	absent	elevate
hesitate	quench	plead	predict
tremble	furnish	companion	tarnish

1. to put off an action because you're unsure of something

____

2. happens every year

____

3. to shake or quiver

____

4. to beg or ask for something using strong emotion

____

5. the study of living things

____

6. a dividing line

____

7. someone a person travels with or spends time with

____

8. spending money wisely and not foolishly

____

9. to lift up or raise higher

____

10. to become dull in color or less bright

____

11. round

____

12. to reduce in size or number

____

13. to satisfy thirst or put out a fire

____

14. from another country

____

15. to provide or supply

____

16. to ask for

____

17. rough; rugged

____

18. setting or surroundings

____

19. to say that something will occur in the future, predict

____

20. not present; missing, absent

____

Greek and Latin affixes and roots

Read each root word, prefix or suffix and then find the definition it matches in the box, and write it in the blank space . If you get stuck, think of words that start with or contain the root word, prefix or suffix.

measure	carry	speech	earth	all	write		
excessive	many	opposite	small	heat	star		
life	bend	body	sound	see	year	not	far

1. geo ___________
2. tele ___________
3. corp ___________
4. meter ___________
5. therm ___________
6. micro ___________
7. multi ___________
8. graph ___________
9. astr ___________
10. bio ___________
11. ann ___________
12. port ___________
13. flex ___________
14. omni ___________
15. vis (vid) ___________
16. logue ___________
17. phone ___________
18. hyper ___________
19. anti ___________
20. non ___________

Similes and Metaphors

Writers describe many things when they write. Some of the tools they use to describe things are adjectives, adverbs, and appositives, which you're already familiar with. They use other tools to describe things, too. Two of their most powerful tools are **similes** and **metaphors**. Similes and metaphors describe something by comparing it to something else. A simile uses the word *like* or the word *as*; a metaphor doesn't. A metaphor simply calls something by another name to make the point. Here is a simile:

Since the air conditioner broke down, it's like an oven in here.

Here is a metaphor:

Without air conditioning, the room turned into an oven.

The first sentence, which contains the simile, says the room is *like* an oven. In the second sentence, the metaphor says the room *is* an oven. Of course, the room isn't really an oven, or even very much like an oven, but the readers understand that the writers are simply using colorful language to make the point that *it's extremely hot in the room*. You'll want to use similes and metaphors in your own writing, too, so it's important to understand them.

Similes and Metaphors Exercise

In each sentence, there is a simile or metaphor. Circle it, and in the blank line below the sentence, write in your own words what point the writer is making with the simile or metaphor.

1. Quiet, mild-mannered Trent turns into a bulldozer on the football field.

____

2. Winning the spelling bee was like a dream come true.

____

3. When the thunderclap hit, Jared became as white as a ghost.

____

4. The Yankees are the 800 pound gorilla of the American League.

____

5. He ate the whole thing all by himself – when it comes to food, he's a vacuum cleaner.

____

6. To me, the sky is like a big blue blanket that keeps the world safe and warm.

____

7. Just like clockwork, my cat emerges from his hiding place twice a day.

____

8. This is delicious, Mrs. Jones – you're a magician in the kitchen!

____

9. After Sam grew six inches, he felt like a giraffe among his classmates.

____

10. You're an angel for helping me with those heavy bags, young man.

____

Idioms and Proverbs

Idioms

There are many phrases people we hear and read quite often that mean something different than what the actual words mean. These are called figures of speech, or idioms. Here is an example:

That math test was a piece of cake.

Of course, the math test wasn't literally a piece of cake. The writer is saying that the test was so easy that taking it was as pleasant as eating a piece of cake. (Many idioms are metaphors, like this one.)

Here's another one:

I was on pins and needles waiting for the judges' decision on Best in Show.

The idiom *on pins and needles* means anxious, worried, or excited about something.

You are already familiar with lots of idioms; people use these figures of speech all the time. In fact, if you listed every idiom you already know and understand, the list would have hundreds of items on it.

Idioms Exercise

Each item contains a common idiom. In the blank line below it, explain what the idiom means.

1. pulling someone's leg

____

2. all bark and no bite

____

3. raining cats and dogs

____

4. hit the sack

____

5. costs an arm and a leg

____

6. blew his top

____

7. couch potato

____

8. walking on eggshells

____

9. hold your horses

____

10. in hot water

____

Proverbs

Proverbs are short sayings that express a truth. Most of them have been around for hundreds of years. People still quote them because of the truths that they contain.

Proverbs Exercise

Fill in the blank space with the word or phrase to complete each proverb.

1. When the cat's away,

____.

2. There's no place like

____.

3. Don't count your chickens

____.

4. Actions speak

____.

5. The early bird

____.

6. One good turn

____.

7. You can't have your cake

____.

8. Don't put all your eggs

____.

9. A fool and his money

____.

10. Beauty is in

____.

Synonyms and Antonyms

Antonyms are words which have opposite meanings. Here are some pairs of antonyms:

hot / cold   tall / short   drab / colorful   illness / health   wealth / poverty

Synonyms are words that have almost the same meaning. Here are some pairs of synonyms:

fast / speedy   fat / pudgy   happy / glad   strange / weird   sour / bitter

Antonym Exercise

Read each word below, then find its antonym in the box at the top, and write it in the blank space next to the word.

shame	stingy	close	inferior	clumsy
seldom	weakness	temporary	slow	hideous
boring	loyalty	liquid	dislike	failure
organized	friendly	dull	folly	rare

1. beautiful ___________

2. superior ___________

3. common ___________

4. generous ___________

5. hostile ___________

6. exciting ___________

7. frequently __________

8. permanent __________

9. treason __________

10. wisdom __________

11. rapid __________

12. graceful __________

13.honor __________

14. success __________

15. solid __________

16. sloppy __________

17. distant __________

18. admire __________

19. brilliant __________

20. strength __________

Synonym Exercise

Read each word below, then find its synonym in the box at the top, and write it in the blank space next to the word.

hilarious	depressed	city	ocean	purchase
powerful	anxious	prize	cyclone	frailty
foolish	intelligent	regal	shrub	squirm
thing	rock	total	sleepy	leap

1. weakness __________

2. royal __________

3. award __________

4. item __________

5. jump __________

6. nervous __________

7. funny __________

8. sad __________

9. bush __________

10. sea __________

11. sum __________

12. tornado __________

13. buy __________

14. strong ___________

15. stone ___________

16. silly ___________

17. fidget ___________

18. town ___________

19. smart ___________

20. drowsy ___________

Opinion Essay

First, choose a topic. Your opinion piece can be about a news report you saw last night, or a book you read recently, or a political subject, or any number of things. Anything that you have a definite opinion about one way or another is a suitable topic. What's important is that you have an opinion about it, and you can express those opinions. So your subject matter is up to you.

Start writing by introducing your topic. Tell the reader what subject you'll be discussing, and state your opinion on the matter. Give reasons for your opinions, and give real details and facts to back up your opinion. Use words and phrases such as *in addition to, therefore, that's why, in order to,* etc. to show how the facts and details relate to your opinion. Finish by writing a conclusion that clearly but briefly sums up your article.

(Organizing hint: many professional writers find it's easier to write an article if they make an outline first, writing down the various points they want to make. This helps them stay focused, and it also helps them make sure they cover everything.)

Informational or Explanatory Essay

In this writing exercise, you'll explain a subject or give information about a topic, so it should be something you're already familiar with. There are lots of things you know about which you could choose for a topic - games, sports, hobbies, your neighborhood, pets, etc. Introduce your topic right off the bat, and tell the reader exactly what aspect of it you'll be writing about. Use details such as quotes, facts, and definitions to make things clearer and more interesting. Use words and phrases such as *and, but, also, too, another, because*, etc., to link different details together. Break your article up into separate paragraphs, and make each paragraph about a certain part of the topic, so your article is organized. Use headings, also called subtitles, above one or more paragraph. Make sure your writing is clear and easy for the reader to understand and follow. Finish up with a good conclusion.

(Organizing hint: many professional writers find it's easier to write an article if they make an outline first, writing down the various points they want to make. This helps them stay focused, and it also helps them make sure they cover everything.)

Tell a Story

Now it's time to show off your creative side by writing a short story. It doesn't have to be fiction, but it does have to be in narrative form. That means it describes an event or experience, either real or made up, with a clear beginning and ending. Start off by describing the setting, to set the scene for the reader. Make it clear if you're writing as a narrator, or one of the characters (and it has to be one or the other, not both). Try hard to describe actions and scenes so that the reader feels like he's right in the middle of the story. Use dialogue to move the action along and reveal more about the characters. Be sure to make it clear when and in what order things happen, too. Close out your story with a conclusion that doesn't leave the reader scratching his head in puzzlement.

(Organizing hint: many professional writers find it's easier to write a story if they make an outline first, writing down the various characters, scenes, and action they want to show. This helps them stay focused, and it also helps them make sure they cover everything.)

Practice Test #1

Practice Questions

Questions 1 - 12pertain to the following story:

The Tournament

(1) The sun was warm as Keith and Joe walked home from school.

(2) "Tomorrow will be a perfect day to skateboard," Keith said. "Let's meet at the park at ten o'clock."

(3) "I can't," Joe said. "I have a karate tournament. I've been doing it since I was six."

(4) "Can't you get out of it?" Keith complained. "This will be the first sunny Saturday of spring."

(5) "I have a better idea. Come with me to the tournament." said Joe.

(6) "It sounds boring," Keith said.

(7) "It won't be boring," Joe promised. "Will you come?"

(8) "I'll ask my mom," Keith said.

(9) Later, Keith called Joe. "Mom said I can go. When will we meet?"

(10) "We'll pick you up at nine o'clock," Joe said. "See you tomorrow!"

(11) On the drive to the tournament, Joe told Keith that karate was a tradition in his family. Joe's father started studying karate

when he was six, just like Joe. His grandfather learned karate as a boy in Okinawa.

(12) "Where's Okinawa?" Keith asked.

(13) "It's an island off the tip of Japan," Joe told him. "That's where my grandfather grew up."

(14) "Is your grandfather your karate teacher?" Keith asked.

(15) Joe laughed. "No. He's too old to teach anymore. I study with Master Lee in a dojo downtown."

(16) Joe explained that a dojo was a karate school. Master Lee taught many students in his dojo. In the tournament, Joe would compete against friends from his dojo and students from other dojos. He was nervous and excited.

(17) When they arrived at the tournament, Master Lee met them near the door. Joe introduced Keith to Master Lee. Master Lee smiled and bowed to Keith. Keith bowed back, even though he felt a little funny.

(18) Master Lee led them into the arena. The wide floor was divided into several rings. In each ring, students competed. Around the rings, family and friends cheered and offered encouragement. Joe waved to friends from his dojo.

(19) "I have to get dressed," Joe told Keith. "I'll be back in a few minutes."

(20) Joe disappeared into a locker room. When he came back, he wore a white top and pants. A green belt was tied around his waist.

(21) Keith grinned. "Nice outfit. Why is your belt green? It seems like everyone here has a different color of belt."

(22) Joe explained that belt color showed the skill level of a student. Beginners had white belts. After passing some tests, they earned a yellow belt. Then they earned a green belt. That was the skill level Joe had achieved. His next step was to earn a brown belt. Someday Joe hoped to earn a black belt like his father and grandfather and Master Lee. Then he could teach karate to others.

(23) Master Lee called Joe to a nearby ring. It was almost time for Joe to compete. He did some stretching exercises to prepare his body for competition. When Joe's name was called, he bowed to Master Lee and walked to the center of the ring.

(24) Keith felt worried. "What if he gets hurt?" Keith asked Joe's dad.

(25) Joe's dad explained it was a light contact competition. Students made only gentle, controlled contact with each other. They were judged on speed and accuracy rather than force or power. Keith was relieved.

(26) As the match began, Keith cheered for Joe as he punched, kicked, and blocked against his opponent's attacks. Joe was really good at karate! Keith's and Joe's dads yelled and clapped as the match came to an end.

(27) Joe was breathless when he came to stand beside them. They waited anxiously for the judges' decision. The four judges conferred quietly at their table. Finally, they announced their decision: all four points went to Joe. Joe won the match!

(28) As the tournament continued, Joe kept winning matches. Keith cheered louder and louder with every win. He felt proud that someone as talented as Joe was his friend. He also admired the way his friend used his karate skills to honor his family's heritage. Keith hoped he could attend another tournament with Joe very soon!

1. In what season is the story set?

Ⓐ Spring

Ⓑ Summer

Ⓒ Fall

Ⓓ Winter

2. What is a dojo?

Ⓐ A karate technique

Ⓑ A karate school

Ⓒ A karate teacher

Ⓓ A karate student

3. In paragraph 27, what is the definition of the word "conferred"?

Ⓐ Argued

Ⓑ Joked

Ⓒ Decided

Ⓓ Discussed

4. Based on the story, why does Joe want Keith to come to the karate tournament with him?

Ⓐ Joe wants Keith to understand that karate is important to him

Ⓑ Joe does not want Keith to go skateboarding without him

Ⓒ Joe wants Keith to meet Master Lee and Joe's dad

Ⓓ Joe wants Keith to be jealous of his karate skills

This question has two parts. Answer Part A, then answer Part B.

5. Part A: Which of the following best describes how Keith's attitude toward the karate tournament changes between paragraph 6 and paragraph 28?

Ⓐ Keith's attitude does not change at all

Ⓑ Keith goes from thinking the tournament is boring to hoping to attend another one

Ⓒ Keith goes from thinking that karate is an awesome sport to thinking that karate is boring

Ⓓ Keith decides he doesn't want to skateboard anymore; he wants to study karate

Part B: Give a sentence that represents how Keith felt about karate earlier in the story, and a sentence that shows how he felt later in the story.

____

____

____

____

6. Complete the following chart based on information in the story:

White belt

Yellow belt

____

Brown belt

Black belt

Ⓐ Blue belt

Ⓑ Green belt

Ⓒ Red belt

Ⓓ Purple belt

This question has two parts. Answer Part A, then answer Part B.

7. Part A: What is the primary purpose of this story?

Ⓐ To show how important karate is to Joe

Ⓑ To show how much Keith likes skateboarding

Ⓒ To show how long Keith and Joe have been friends

Ⓓ To show what a good teacher Master Lee is

Part B: Which sentence or sentences from the story supports your answer from Part A?

Ⓐ Joe introduced Keith to Master Lee.

Ⓑ "I can't," Joe said. "I have a karate tournament. I've been doing it since I was six."

Ⓒ "Tomorrow will be a perfect day to skateboard," Keith said.

Ⓓ Keith hoped he could attend another tournament with Joe very soon!

8. Based on the information given in the story, how likely is Joe to keep practicing karate?

Ⓐ Very unlikely

Ⓑ Somewhat unlikely

Ⓒ Somewhat likely

Ⓓ Very likely

This question has two parts. Answer Part A, then answer Part B.

9. Part A: Which of the following statements about the story is a fact?

Ⓐ By the end of the story, Keith wants to take karate

Ⓑ Because Joe wins all his matches, Master Lee is obviously an excellent teacher

Ⓒ Joe's father and grandfather both practice karate

Ⓓ None of the other students in Master Lee's dojo are as good as Joe

Part B: Which sentence or sentences from the story supports your answer from Part A?

Ⓐ Joe kept winning matches.

Ⓑ He felt proud that someone as talented as Joe was his friend.

Ⓒ Finally, they announced their decision: all four points went to Joe. Joe won the match!

Ⓓ Joe's father started studying karate when he was six, just like Joe. His grandfather learned karate as a boy in Okinawa.

10. Based on the story, how does practicing karate honor Joe's family heritage?

Ⓐ Karate is taught in Okinawa, and Joe's grandfather is Okinawan

Ⓑ Karate is a tradition in Joe's family, practiced by three generations

Ⓒ Karate is popular in the town where Joe and his family live

Ⓓ Many Asians practice karate, and Joe is Asian

11. Write a brief summary of the story.

____

____

____

____

12. What color belt is required to teach Karate?

Ⓐ Blue belt

Ⓑ Green belt

Ⓒ Black belt

Ⓓ Purple belt

Questions 13 - 27 pertain to the following passages:

Remember the Alamo

(1) In the early 1700s, the Spanish established missions throughout the land we now know as the state of Texas. One of the most famous of these missions was San Antonio de Valero, better known by its nickname: the Alamo. This was the most successful mission in the area, and it served a number of purposes for the surrounding communities.

(2) For over a century, the Alamo served as an active mission. Church services were held in the cool, shady buildings, providing welcome relief from the blazing summer sun. Couples were married at the Alamo. Babies were baptized there. The Alamo also served as a trading post, supply depot, and communication center. In later years, however, the Alamo served its most famous and—arguably—most important role; it was a fortress for freedom fighters.

(3) During the 1830s, Texas was in a battle for independence from Mexico, which owned it at that time. This struggle came to a head in 1836 when 184 Texans, led by William Travis, holed up in the Alamo. Travis and other famous American fighters—including Jim Bowie and Davy Crockett—fought side by side with farmers, ranchers, cowboys, and businessmen. Those brave men held off Mexican General Santa Anna's army for 13 days from the secure walls of the Alamo.

(4) Finally, in the gray, early morning light of March 6, 1836, General Santa Anna and an army of 4,000 soldiers overran the Alamo. Every man in the Alamo died that day, but their ability to

hold out for nearly two weeks gave American General Sam Houston the time he needed to assemble a more substantial army. General Houston soon defeated General Santa Anna, and Texas won its independence, thanks in great part to the brave men who defended the Alamo and the cause of freedom.

A Day at the Alamo

(1) Just before spring break, Eric's class took a trip to visit the Alamo. Before they left, they read about William Travis, Jim Bowie, and Davy Crockett in their history books. They also read about General Santa Anna and his army. Eric couldn't wait to see the place where the actual battle for the Alamo occurred.

(2) Eric watched buildings roll by as the school bus drove into downtown San Antonio. Near the River Walk, the bus stopped and the class climbed out.

(3) "Stay together, please," Mrs. Morgan, Eric's teacher, directed the class. "After I check us in, we will go listen to a history talk."

(4) A few minutes later, Mrs. Morgan led the class to a patio area. A guide met them there and told the story of the Alamo, from its establishment by the Spanish to the famous standoff and battle in 1836. Eric listened carefully. He wanted to remember all the details to help him complete the History Hunt worksheet Mrs. Morgan had given them.

(5) When the history talk was over, Mrs. Morgan divided the class into small groups. Each group was assigned a parent volunteer and given an hour to complete a self-tour of the Alamo and the grounds. During that time, they were supposed to look for all the necessary answers to complete their History Hunt worksheets. In an hour, all groups would meet at the gift shop.

(6) Eric loved walking through the old buildings and viewing the artifacts. He liked the gardens and the Long Barrack Museum, but his favorite building was the Shrine. He especially liked the old bell that was kept in a small room in the Shrine. Eric could imagine Davy Crockett himself ringing that bell!

(7) Soon the hour was up, and Eric's group headed for the gift shop. While there, Eric used his allowance to buy a book about Davy Crockett and a small Texas flag. Back on the bus, Eric waved his flag proudly at passing cars. He knew he would always remember the Alamo.

Use the story "Remember the Alamo" to answer questions 14-19

13. What was the official name of the mission nicknamed "the Alamo"?

Ⓐ San Antonio de Valente

Ⓑ San Antonio de Verde

Ⓒ San Antonio de Valero

Ⓓ San Antonio de Vallejo

14. Which of the following represents the author's main purpose in writing this story?

Ⓐ To inform

Ⓑ To influence

Ⓒ To entertain

Ⓓ To persuade

15. What was the main motivation for the men who fought at the Alamo?

Ⓐ Wealth

Ⓑ Fame

Ⓒ Safety

Ⓓ Freedom

16. Based on the information in paragraph 2, what was the purpose of the Alamo?

Ⓐ It was designed as a war fortress

Ⓑ It was designed to serve many purposes in the community

Ⓒ It was designed as a trading post

Ⓓ It was designed as a saloon

17. Which of the following is a statement of opinion?

Ⓐ William Travis, Davy Crockett, and Jim Bowie fought at the Alamo

Ⓑ All the men who fought to defend the Alamo died in the battle

Ⓒ General Santa Anna was eventually defeated by General Sam Houston

Ⓓ General Santa Anna was a better leader than William Travis

18. How many Americans died while defending the Alamo?

Ⓐ 184

Ⓑ 13

Ⓒ 136

Ⓓ 47

19. Which of the following people participated in the battle of the Alamo? Select all that apply.

I. General Sam Houston
II. Davy Crockett
III. Jim Bowie
IV. General Santa Anna
V. Andrew Jackson

Use the story "A Day at the Alamo" to answer questions 20-25

20. Where does the story say the Alamo is located?

Ⓐ Just outside San Antonio

Ⓑ Near the San Antonio River

Ⓒ In downtown San Antonio

Ⓓ Across the river from San Antonio

21. Which artifact was Eric's favorite during his trip to the Alamo?

Ⓐ The Texas flag

Ⓑ The old bell

Ⓒ The Long Barrack Museum

Ⓓ The gardens

22. Complete the following schedule for Eric's class trip:

1. Arrive at the Alamo and check in
2. Attend history talk on the patio
3. Divide into groups for self-tour
4. ______________________

Ⓐ Meet in the gardens

Ⓑ Meet on the patio

Ⓒ Meet at the gift shop

Ⓓ Meet at the bus

23. Why was Eric so excited about visiting the Alamo?

Ⓐ He wanted to see where the battle occurred

Ⓑ He heard there were interesting items in the gift shop

Ⓒ He enjoyed riding on the school bus

Ⓓ His friends were excited about the trip

24. In paragraph 6, what is the best definition of the word "artifacts"?

Ⓐ Buildings

Ⓑ Historical items

Ⓒ Documents and pictures

Ⓓ Furnishings

This question has two parts. Answer Part A, then answer Part B.

25. Part A: Which paragraph tells the most about Eric's favorite experiences at the Alamo?

Ⓐ Paragraph 4

Ⓑ Paragraph 5

Ⓒ Paragraph 6

Ⓓ Paragraph 7

Part B: Which sentence supports your answer from Part A?

Ⓐ He especially liked the old bell that was kept in a small room in the Shrine.

Ⓑ When the history talk was over, Mrs. Morgan divided the class into small groups.

Ⓒ While there, Eric used his allowance to buy a book about Davy Crockett and a small Texas flag.

Ⓓ Eric listened carefully.

Use both "Remember the Alamo" and "A Day at the Alamo" to answer questions 26 and 27.

26. What theme is central to both of these stories, joining them together?

Ⓐ Love of freedom

Ⓑ Davy Crockett

Ⓒ Independence of Texas

Ⓓ History of the Alamo

27. Which of the following represents the biggest difference between the stories?

Ⓐ One involves a school class and the other doesn't

Ⓑ The Alamo changed a lot between the two stories

Ⓒ One is nonfiction and the other is fiction

Ⓓ One involves General Santa Anna and the other doesn't

Questions 28-40 pertain to the following passage:

A Lesson Learned

(1) Beautiful melodies floated from Uncle Eddie's guitar. Kari listened with wonder. The way Uncle Eddie made the guitar sing filled Kari with a desire to learn to play. She wanted to make beautiful music too.

(2) "Teach me to play, Uncle Eddie," Kari begged.

(3) Uncle Eddie looked intently at Kari. "Learning to play isn't easy, Kari. It takes hard work and practice. Are you ready for that?"

(4) "I am! I promise." Kari was thrilled. She was sure playing the guitar would come easily for her. "When can we start?"

(5) "I'll come by at two o'clock on Saturday," Uncle Eddie said. "Be ready to work hard."

(6) Kari laughed. "I will," she promised. "Thanks, Uncle Eddie. See you Saturday!"

(7) Kari could hardly wait for Saturday to come. She dreamed about the songs she would play. She imagined impressing her friends with her skills. Kari was sure she would be a guitar expert in no time. She was so excited.

(8) On Saturday afternoon, Uncle Eddie rang the doorbell. Kari ran to let him in.

(9) "Ready to learn?" Uncle Eddie greeted her.

(10) Kari nodded. She followed him into the family room. She waited for him to get out his guitar and teach her a song, but he didn't even open the case. Instead, he took a book from his music bag.

(11) "We'll start with a history of the guitar," Uncle Eddie said. "Did you know stringed instruments have been around for thousands of years?"

(12) Kari was unimpressed. "Wow," she said.

(13) Uncle Eddie said guitars came from Spain more than 500 years ago. He said they could be used to play a variety of music styles and were one of the most popular instruments.

(14) Kari sighed. "That's great, Uncle Eddie, but I just want to play. When can I start playing songs?"

(15) Uncle Eddie laughed. "Patience, Kari. There's a lot to learn about the guitar before you're ready to play one."

(16) "Like what?" Kari asked.

(17) Uncle Eddie handed her a diagram of a guitar. He explained the two basic guitar parts were the body and the neck. These were made up of other parts.

(18) "The tuning pegs are tightened and loosened so the strings make the right notes," Uncle Eddie told Kari.

(19) Then he showed her the nut at the top and the bridge at the bottom that held the strings in place. He pointed out the fingerboard all along the neck and the frets that helped with finger placement. Finally, he described the top of the body—the sounding board—with a hole in the middle to produce a sweet sound.

(20) Uncle Eddie told Kari to learn the names of the guitar parts as her homework for the next lesson.

(21) "But I don't want homework," Kari protested. "I want to play songs! I didn't even play one note."

(22) With a sigh, Uncle Eddie opened his guitar case and took out his instrument. He played a simple folk song. When he played the song three times, Kari grinned.

(23) "I've got it! I can do this," Kari insisted.

(24) Uncle Eddie showed her how to hold the guitar. Kari started to play, but the notes were all wrong. It didn't sound at all like Uncle Eddie's beautiful music. Kari handed the guitar back to Uncle Eddie with frustration.

(25) "Maybe the guitar isn't for me," she said.

(26) Without a word, Uncle Eddie took out a CD and put it in the player behind him. Tuneless, horrible music filled the room. Kari laughed.

(27) "Hey! That person is worse than I am," she said.

(28) Uncle Eddie smiled. "That's me at my first lesson."

(29) "No way!" Kari said.

(30) "Yep," said Uncle Eddie. "Kari, I've played for 15 years. It took time and practice to get this good."

(31) "Do you think I could play like you someday?" Kari asked.

(32) "If you work hard," answered Uncle Eddie.

(33) "Maybe I should start with my homework for our next lesson," Kari said.

(34) Uncle Eddie hugged her. "That sounds like a great place to start."

28. Based on the story, which of the following best qualifies Uncle Eddie to teach guitar lessons to Kari?

Ⓐ He is Kari's uncle

Ⓑ He has taught many guitar students before

Ⓒ He is looking for work

Ⓓ He knows how to play the guitar very well

29. Which part of the guitar is used to help strings make the right notes?

Ⓐ Tuning pegs

Ⓑ Fingerboard

Ⓒ Bridge

Ⓓ Soundboard

30. In paragraph 3, what does the word "intently" mean?

Ⓐ In a focused way

Ⓑ In a disinterested way

Ⓒ In a happy way

Ⓓ In a disgusted way

31. Which of the following belongs in the empty box according to the sequence of the story?

Kari wants to learn to play the guitar.	Uncle Eddie agrees to teach her.		Kari becomes bored and frustrated.	Kari learns it takes hard work to play guitar.

Ⓐ Kari plays well on her first try

Ⓑ Uncle Eddie begins the lesson with the history and structure of the guitar

Ⓒ Uncle Eddie does not show up for the lesson

Ⓓ Kari's friends decide they want Uncle Eddie to teach them too

32. What is the main theme of this story?

Ⓐ To show that Uncle Eddie is not a good teacher

Ⓑ To show that Kari is not a good student

Ⓒ To show that learning to play the guitar is boring

Ⓓ To show that learning to play the guitar takes hard work

33. In what point of view is this story written?

Ⓐ First person

Ⓑ Second person

Ⓒ Third person

Ⓓ All of the above

34. What is the difference between Uncle Eddie's feelings and Kari's feelings about learning to play the guitar?

Ⓐ Uncle Eddie feels it will be hard, while Kari feels it will be easy

Ⓑ Kari feels it will be hard, while Uncle Eddie feels it will be easy

Ⓒ Both Kari and Uncle Eddie feel it will be hard

Ⓓ Both Kari and Uncle Eddie feel it will be easy

35. How does the author show in paragraph 14 that Kari is unhappy with Uncle Eddie's history lesson on guitars?

Ⓐ By saying, "Kari was unhappy."

Ⓑ By having Kari say something unkind to Uncle Eddie

Ⓒ By writing, "Kari sighed."

Ⓓ By having Kari leave the room

36. Who is playing the "horrible music" Kari hears in paragraph 26?

Ⓐ Uncle Eddie's first student

Ⓑ Uncle Eddie

Ⓒ Kari

Ⓓ Kari's father

37. Based on the information presented in the story, which of the following is a fact instead of an opinion?

Ⓐ Uncle Eddie has been playing guitar for 15 years

Ⓑ Kari will never learn to be a good guitar player

Ⓒ Playing the guitar is a boring hobby

Ⓓ Everyone who plays the guitar knows a lot about guitar history

38. As used in paragraph 19, what does the word "bridge" mean?

Ⓐ a passage way over something

Ⓑ a piece of wood that supports guitar strings

Ⓒ a way to play the guitar

Ⓓ a way to hold the guitar

39. List four parts of a guitar below.

1. ______________________________

2. ______________________________

3. ______________________________

4. ______________________________

40. In what paragraph did it seem like Kari had given up on guitar?

Ⓐ paragraph 14

Ⓑ paragraph 25

Ⓒ paragraph 29

Ⓓ paragraph 31

Practice Test #2

Practice Questions

Questions 1 - 11 pertain to the following passage:

<u>That Was Then, and This Is Now</u>

(1) Becca slumped on Grandma's flowered sofa. She loved Grandma, but her house was so dull. Becca was bored.

(2) "Grandma, there's nothing to do!" Becca whined.

(3) "You could watch TV," Grandma suggested.

(4) "There's nothing to watch on your channels. Why don't you have cable?" Becca asked.

(5) "I don't need cable," Grandma said. "When I was little, there were only three television stations available. In fact, we didn't even have a TV until I was 12 years old. And even then, it was black-and-white."

(6) "That sounds awful," Becca said.

(7) "Actually, we thought it was wonderful," Grandma said. "But that was then, and this is now."

(8) "Well, what about getting a game system or a computer. That would give me something to do when I'm here," Becca said.

(9) "We didn't have computers or game systems when I was young," Grandma said. "But we always managed to keep ourselves quite busy."

(10) "You must have been so bored all the time," Becca said. "What did you do to keep busy?"

(11) "Oh, we played outside. We rode our bikes, and sometimes we stuck playing cards in the spokes of the wheels to make them sound like motorcycles. We went fishing and built forts out of blankets or scrap wood or whatever else we could find. Yes, we kept busy." Grandma smiled, remembering.

(12) "I guess that doesn't sound so bad," Becca said. "But what if it was raining, like today? Then you couldn't do any of those things."
(13) "On rainy days, we played inside games," Grandma said. "We played checkers and solitaire and other games. We read books for hours. We made paper dolls and designed whole wardrobes for them. But I guess that was then, and this is now."
(14) "Wow," said Becca. "That sounds kind of fun. What else was different way back then?"
(15) Grandma laughed. "It wasn't all that long ago, Becca. But many things were different."
(16) Grandma told Becca about having fresh milk delivered to her doorstep in glass bottles instead of buying it in plastic jugs at the supermarket. She talked about wearing dresses to school every day instead of jeans and T-shirts. She talked about using pay phones instead of cell phones. She talked about listening to soap operas on the radio instead of watching them on TV. She talked about playing records and dancing the twist.
(17) "But that was then," Grandma said, "and this is now."
(18) Becca was amazed. "You're right, Grandma. Practically everything is different now. It seems like the whole world has changed since you were my age."
(19) Grandma shook her head. "Not everything has changed, Becca. Some things will never change."
(20) "Like what?" Becca asked.
(21) "Well," Grandma answered, "back then grandmas loved their granddaughters, just like I love you now."
(22) Becca leaned over and hugged Grandma tightly. "I love you, too," she said. "Now, how about a game of checkers?"
(23) Grandma smiled. "Sounds good. Maybe things haven't changed so much after all!"
(24) They played checkers, and Grandma beat Becca all three games. Then they used pillows and blankets and all six dining room chairs to build a massive fort in the living room. They sat in the dim fort and had a picnic lunch of sandwiches and

chocolate chip cookies. After lunch, Grandma showed Becca how to make paper dolls and design clothes for them. The afternoon flew past.

(25) When Becca's mom came to pick her up, Becca did not want to go home.

(26) "But I thought you were bored," Grandma said.

(27) Becca grinned. "Oh, Grandma," she said, "I was bored. But that was then, and this is now!"

1. Where does this story take place?

Ⓐ At Becca's house

Ⓑ At Grandma's house

Ⓒ At a vacation house

Ⓓ At Becca's mom's house

2. Which of the following best represents the main theme of this story?

Ⓐ There are many different ways to have fun

Ⓑ Becca is bored all the time

Ⓒ Grandma is old and dull

Ⓓ Activities from the past are not exciting

3. What word does the author use in paragraph 1 to describe Becca's feelings about Grandma's house?

Ⓐ Exciting

Ⓑ Tolerable

Ⓒ Dull

Ⓓ Boring

This question has two parts. Answer Part A then answer Part B.

4. Part A: What is the difference between Becca's attitude at the beginning of the story and her attitude at the end?

Ⓐ There is no difference in her attitude

Ⓑ She is bored at the beginning of the story and not bored at the end

Ⓒ She is angry with Grandma at the beginning of the story and happy with her at the end

Ⓓ She is excited at the beginning of the story and bored at the end

Part B: What makes her change her attitude?

Ⓐ Nothing, she has no attitude change.

Ⓑ Grandma makes her lunch

Ⓒ Grandma tells her about all the fun things she did as a kid.

Ⓓ Grandma takes her home

5. Which of the following does the story say Grandma did to keep busy when she was young? Select all that apply.

I. Use a computer
II. Play outside
III. Went fishing
IV. Watch color TV
V. Build a fort

6. What is the author's main purpose in writing this story?

Ⓐ To entertain

Ⓑ To inform

Ⓒ To persuade

Ⓓ To influence

7. Which of the following is a statement of fact?

Ⓐ Black-and-white TV is boring

Ⓑ Grandma is a dull person

Ⓒ Milk used to be delivered in glass bottles

Ⓓ Playing outside is exciting

8. Where do Grandma and Becca eat their lunch in this story?

Ⓐ Outside on the lawn

Ⓑ In a blanket fort

Ⓒ At the dining table

Ⓓ At a restaurant

This question has two parts. Answer Part A then answer Part B.

9. Part A: Which of the following does Becca ask Grandma to get in this story?

Ⓐ A dog

Ⓑ A TV

Ⓒ A car

Ⓓ A computer

Part B: What was Grandma's reason for not getting one?

Ⓐ They were too expensive

Ⓑ They were too much upkeep

Ⓒ She didn't have one when she was younger

Ⓓ She just didn't want one

10. Which character in this story has the most positive attitude?

Ⓐ Becca

Ⓑ Grandma

Ⓒ Becca's mom

Ⓓ No one in the story has a positive attitude

11. Which paragraph is the first to show a definite change in Becca's attitude?

Ⓐ Paragraph 10

Ⓑ Paragraph 22

Ⓒ Paragraph 24

Ⓓ Paragraph 26

Questions 12 - 27 pertain to the passages:

The Tradition of Dance

(1) It is estimated that there are over 300 Native American tribes, and each of them uses dancing to communicate culture. Native American dances date back hundreds of years and come in many different forms. Different tribes use dance for different purposes and to convey different messages.

(2) Although each dance is different, they all have meanings that are rooted in ancient tradition. The Iroquois performed a corn husk dance to bring good crops and many healthy babies to the tribe. The Choctaw women danced with medicine men to bring their tribe victory in sporting events. The Plains Indians

offered thanks to the gods through their Sun Dance, and the Cherokee celebrated both peace and war with the Eagle Dance. During the Snake Ceremonial, Hopi dancers even held live snakes in their mouths before releasing them into the desert to bring rain and a good harvest.

(3) Each of the many different dances also requires a unique costume. These costumes vary widely, but—just like the dances—each has a special meaning. Most dance costumes include a headdress and special ceremonial clothing. Some also include a wand, jewelry, and even body paint. In addition, feathers are often used in costumes to symbolize human traits. One of the most common feathers used is the eagle feather, which represents strength in many tribes.

(4) Though many of the Native American dances are now performed only in ceremonies and at powwows, they remain an important element of Native American culture. These dances are a language, rich in history and meaning. They are passed from generation to generation and will always be a vital part of Native American tradition.

The Story of My People

(1) As we pulled into the community college parking lot, I felt my excitement rising. Powwows were one of my favorite things. I loved the talking, the laughing, the music, and—most of all—the dancing. I loved seeing and hearing and feeling my Cherokee heritage.

(2) Inside the large gymnasium, the powwow was just getting started. My father and grandfather went to join the men who had gathered in the far corner. Around the edges of the gym, women sat behind long tables draped with vibrant cloths. On the tables were items for sale. I wandered around and looked at the leather vests, beaded belts, and beautiful jewelry.

(3) As I came to the end of the tables, I heard behind me the low, pulsing beat of a single drum. It made a hollow, echoing sound. Soon other drums joined the rhythm, filling the air with

their deep sound. High-pitched rattles joined in, and a group of men drifted to the center of the floor. The dancing had begun.

(4) I found a seat on some bleachers and watched with wonder. Synchronized steps beat out a perfect rhythm while voices chanted high and low in beautiful unison. Feathers and beads and shiny black braids flashed past as the intensity increased. It was magical to me.

(5) Some dances were for the children; some were for the men or women; some were for everyone. Sometimes tribes danced separately, and sometimes they all danced together. Some dances offered thanks, and others asked for blessings; some were celebrations, and others were prayers. But although each dance was different, they all told a story. It was an ancient story: the story of my people.

Questions 12 - 17pertain to the passage "The Tradition of Dance":

12. How many tribes does the story refer to by name?

Ⓐ 3

Ⓑ 5

Ⓒ 7

Ⓓ 8

13. What is the main purpose of dance in the Native American culture?

Ⓐ To provide exercise

Ⓑ To communicate a message

Ⓒ To entertain children

Ⓓ To prepare for battle

14. According to paragraph 2, what is the similarity between the Iroquois corn husk dance and the Hopi Snake Ceremonial?

Ⓐ They were both intended to bring good crops

Ⓑ They both involved women and medicine men

Ⓒ They both involved the use of snakes

Ⓓ They both involved the use of corn husks

15. Which of the following statements are facts? Select all that apply.

I. Many Native American costumes include a wand and jewelry
II. The dances are passed from generation to generation
III. Ceremonial headdresses make dancers look important
IV. These dances date back hundreds of years
V. Eagle feathers are the best feathers

16. What does the eagle feather represent in many Native American tribes?

Ⓐ Power

Ⓑ Wealth

Ⓒ Strength

Ⓓ Authority

17. What was the author's main purpose in writing this article?

Ⓐ To inform

Ⓑ To entertain

Ⓒ To influence

Ⓓ To persuade

Questions 18- 24 pertain to the passage: "The Story of My People"

18. What tribe represents the heritage of the narrator of this story?

Ⓐ Hopi

Ⓑ Cherokee

Ⓒ Iroquois

Ⓓ Choctaw

19. In what point of view is this story written?

Ⓐ First person

Ⓑ Second person

Ⓒ Third person

Ⓓ None of the above

20. What is the main theme of this story?

Ⓐ Native American dancing tells a story

Ⓑ Powwows are exciting

Ⓒ Community colleges are great places to hold powwows

Ⓓ Native American children learn to dance at a young age

21. Which of the following is a statement of opinion?

Ⓐ Some dances are designed to bring a blessing

Ⓑ Each dance is different, but each has a meaning

Ⓒ Many dances involve synchronized steps, music, and chanting

Ⓓ Native American dancing is emotionally powerful

22. What does the narrator do before the dancing begins?

Ⓐ Buys snacks at the snack bar

Ⓑ Looks at the tables of items for sale

Ⓒ Takes a walk around the campus

Ⓓ Practices different dancing steps

23. What is the meaning of the word "pulsing" as it appears in paragraph 3?

Ⓐ a steady or rhythmic beat

Ⓑ a sudden loud noise

Ⓒ the seeds of a plant

Ⓓ a beating heart

24. The narrator says that the dancing tells a story. What was that story?

Ⓐ the story of the eagle

Ⓑ the story of his people

Ⓒ the story of great harvest

Ⓓ the story of happiness

Questions 25- 27 pertain to both passages "The Tradition of Dance" and "The Story of My People"

25. What main theme is central to both stories?

Ⓐ The value of powwows in Native American culture

Ⓑ The focus on family in Native American culture

Ⓒ The importance of dancing in Native American culture

Ⓓ The power of medicine men in Native American culture

26. What is Native American dancing compared to in both stories?

Ⓐ Language

Ⓑ Music

Ⓒ Cooking

Ⓓ Art

27. Which tribe was mentioned in both stories?

Ⓐ Choctaw

Ⓑ Hopi

Ⓒ Cherokee

Ⓓ Iroquois

Questions 28 - 40 pertain to the following passage:

In Abuela's World

(1) In June, just after school ended, Marianna and her family went to see her abuela—her grandmother—in Tampico, Mexico. By the time they reached Abuela's small house by the sea, Marianna was exhausted. Abuela put a thick mat on the floor for a bed, and Marianna stretched out and went to sleep.

(2) When Marianna awoke the next morning, the sun was already high in the sky. The air was warm and sticky. Marianna rubbed her eyes and wandered into Abuela's kitchen. Delicious smells bubbled up from a pot on the stove.

(3) "Buenos dias, sleepyhead," Abuela said with a grin. "You must have been tired. You slept half the day away."

(4) Marianna stretched and yawned as her mother came into the kitchen. "What are we doing today, Mami?" Marianna asked.

(5) "Papi and Jorge and I are going down to the beach soon," Mami answered. "You can come with us or stay here with Abuela."

(6) Marianna chose the beach. As she lay in the sun, she listened to the waves. Sea birds called overhead, and the gentle sea breeze kissed her face. It was a perfect afternoon.

(7) The next day, Abuela joined them as they drove south to visit some Aztec ruins. Although the Aztec people once ruled the area of Mexico where Abuela lived, they were conquered by the Spaniards long ago. Crumbling ruins were all that remained of their ancient civilization. Marianna had read about the Aztecs in school. It was amazing to think these stones were once part of the great Aztec empire.

(8) On her third full day in Mexico, Marianna saw her cousins. The three boys shyly greeted Marianna. Then they turned to her younger brother, Jorge.

(9) "Want to play some futbol, Jorge?" they asked.

(10) Jorge nodded. He knew futbol meant soccer in Spanish, and he loved soccer. Marianna went out to watch the boys play. She liked soccer, too, but it was too hot to play in the blazing sun.

(11) Marianna sat on the shady porch and watched the boys kick the ball in the dusty street. The boys played hard, and Marianna found herself cheering for Jorge's team. As the sun went down, they called it a tie and finally headed inside.

(12) The visit to Abuela's world flew by. On the day before she had to leave, Marianna found Abuela in the kitchen.

(13) "I don't want to go home," Marianna said. "I love you, and I love Mexico."

(14) Abuela smiled. "I love you, too. But you would eventually miss your life in America. And you can always come to visit."

(15) "I guess so," said Marianna. "But I'll miss Mexico."

(16) "I know," said Abuela, taking Marianna's hand. "So to help you take Mexico with you, we are having a grand fiesta tonight. Come shopping with me."

(17) They went to the open market where vendors spread their goods on blankets on the ground. Abuela selected items for the party, greeting many of the vendors by name. Then she bought Marianna some chicle, Mexican gum made from sapodilla pulp.

(18) That night, dozens of neighbors, friends, and family members came to the party. They talked and laughed and

danced to the mariachi music. Abuela made incredible food for everyone. There was chicken with sweet and spicy mole, enchiladas with rich sauce, rice, fruit, and plenty of tortillas. It was a true feast.

(19) The party went late into the night. Marianna felt she had barely slept when Papi shook her awake and told her it was time to go. As they drove away, Marianna waved to Abuela. Although she was going home, Marianna knew her heart would always hold a special place for Abuela's world.

28. What is the Spanish word for grandmother?

Ⓐ Amiga

Ⓑ Abuela

Ⓒ Alla

Ⓓ Alegra

29. Where is the main setting for this story?

Ⓐ In the southwest

Ⓑ In Tampico, Mexico

Ⓒ At the ruins

Ⓓ In the open market

30. Which choice best finishes the following chart of events on Marianna's vacation?

Marianna goes to the beach.	Marianna visits the ruins.	Marianna sees her cousins.	Marianna visits the open market	

Ⓐ Marianna visits a mountain

Ⓑ Marianna takes a road trip through Mexico

Ⓒ Marianna attends a big party at her grandmother's house

Ⓓ Marianna watches the boys play soccer

This question has two parts. Answer Part A then answer Part B.

31. Part A: Which paragraphs discuss Marianna's visit with her cousins?

Ⓐ Paragraph 5 through paragraph 9

Ⓑ Paragraph 6 through paragraph 10

Ⓒ Paragraph 7 through paragraph 10

Ⓓ Paragraph 8 through paragraph 11

Part B: Based on your answer from Part A which event also happened in these paragraphs?

Ⓐ Marianna visited the beach

Ⓑ Jorge played soccer with his cousins

Ⓒ Marianna and her family visited the Aztec ruins

Ⓓ Marianna and Abuela went to the market

32. Which word is the best English translation for the Spanish word "futbol"?

Ⓐ Football

Ⓑ Soccer

Ⓒ Baseball

Ⓓ Kickball

33. Why did the author tell this story from Marianna's point of view?

Ⓐ So the reader can understand Marianna's thoughts and feelings

Ⓑ Because there was no other main character in the story

Ⓒ Because all good stories are written in third-person point of view

Ⓓ This story is not written from Marianna's point of view

34. Why does the story say Marianna doesn't want to leave Mexico?

Ⓐ She hates the long trip

Ⓑ She doesn't have to go to school in Mexico

Ⓒ She loves her grandmother, and she loves Mexico

Ⓓ She likes the weather at the beach

35. In paragraph 6, which literary device is used to describe the wind?

Ⓐ Simile

Ⓑ Personification

Ⓒ Metaphor

Ⓓ No literary device is used

This question has two parts. Answer Part A then answer Part B.

36. Part A: Which word best describes the relationship between Marianna and her grandmother?

Ⓐ Tense

Ⓑ Distant

Ⓒ Polite

Ⓓ Loving

Part B: Give an example that supports your answer from Part A.

____

____

____

37. Which of the following is a statement of opinion?

Ⓐ Grandmother made chicken with mole for the party

Ⓑ Mariachi music was played at the party

Ⓒ The food at the party was incredible

Ⓓ Neighbors, friends, and family members attended the party

38. Where did Marianna go with her grandmother on the day of the party?

Ⓐ To the open market

Ⓑ To the beach

Ⓒ To the ruins

Ⓓ To the supermarket

39. According to the story, what is the main ingredient of chicle?

Ⓐ Chicken

Ⓑ Chocolate

Ⓒ Sugar and spices

Ⓓ Sapodilla pulp

40. When did the boys stop playing soccer?

Ⓐ When it was time to eat

Ⓑ When it was time for bed

Ⓒ When one team scored five goals

Ⓓ When the sun went down

Thank You

We at Mometrix would like to extend our heartfelt thanks to you, our friend and patron, for allowing us to play a part in your journey. It is a privilege to serve people from all walks of life who are unified in their commitment to building the best future they can for themselves.

The preparation you devote to these important testing milestones may be the most valuable educational opportunity you have for making a real difference in your life. We encourage you to put your heart into it—that feeling of succeeding, overcoming, and yes, conquering will be well worth the hours you've invested.

We want to hear your story, your struggles and your successes, and if you see any opportunities for us to improve our materials so we can help others even more effectively in the future, please share that with us as well. **The team at Mometrix would be absolutely thrilled to hear from you!** So please, send us an email (support@mometrix.com) and let's stay in touch.

Online Resources

Due to our efforts to try to keep this book to a manageable length, we've created a link that will give you access to all of your online resources:

mometrix.com/resources719/ssncg4elarwb

It's Your Moment, Let's Celebrate It!

Share your story @mometrixtestpreparation

TABLE OF CONTENTS

Workbook Answers

Reading: Literature & Foundational Skills

The Alligator and the Squirrel answers

1. c
2. It was astonishing because it was very dangerous -- the alligator was very likely to catch the squirrel and eat him.
3. c
4. d
5. He let the squirrel go as a reward for making him laugh when he suggested that a tiny squirrel could help a mighty alligator
6. b
7. ne glect ed
8. a
9. b
10. a

Audrey's Braces answers

1. She thinks they will make her ugly and that other kids will ridicule her and won't want to be her friend.
2. four
3. c
4. Trojans
5. Audrey
6. Audrey's dad
7. d
8. (answers will vary) she was so happy that her friends still liked her and she wasn't going to be an outcast that she forgot about the little bit of physical pain she had.
9. e ven tu al ly
10. a

The Big Cupcake Heist answers

1. c
2. The word *heist* usually means a robbery of something very valuable, and the word *great* implies a big event, too, but since we're also told that it's all about a cupcake, we know the author is being humorous.
3. b
4. She is being **sarcastic**, which means she is saying the opposite of what she really means.
5. perfect pumpkin pastries
6. b
7. You would stress them more than the rest of the words.
8. c
9. a real mystery
10. Probably because she knew who ate the cupcake
11. He was making a joke about Jack being dressed like a pirate and Jaci being dressed like a nurse.

Anna Beth's Birthday Party answers

1. d
2. b
3. Because she knew it was Anna Beth's dad at the door
4. accomplish – it means to do, achieve, make happen, etc.
5. answers will vary

Josh's Big Game answers

1. ant i ci pa tion
2. c
3. d
4. a
5. d
6. un der es ti mat ed
7. c

8. it means they looked at each other at the same time
9. (answers will vary) they were concerned because Josh wanted to get back into the game and they wanted to make sure that didn't happen | they were each waiting for the other to speak | they knew how disappointed Josh was and wanted to choose their words carefully |
10. c
11. the fact that it was the conference championship game
12. d
13. Yes, because he can't wait 'til next year.
14. Dr. Huff
15. b

Meagan's Trip answers

1. The first meaning refers to the trip Meagan is taking to go hiking on Mount Ellis. The second meaning refers to her tripping over the root and breaking her arm.
2. Happy Valley Humane Society
3. animal doctor
4. vet er i nar i an
5. b
6. dry runs
7. a
8. c
9. She fell and broke her arm because she was running so fast she didn't notice the root and tripped over it. She was running in order to catch up to the others because she had stayed behind to take a photo.
10. preventing
11. (several possible answers)
each takes place during an outdoor athletic event (football game, hike)
main character suffers serious injury
characters are mainly young people
each involves a group of friends (football team, Girl Scout troop)
a long awaited day doesn't turn out the way the person had hoped it would

the main character is sad at first after being injured, but later cheers up thanks to friends
the main characters find out how much their friends care about them
12. The difference was that they were playing in a conference game, for the season championship. They couldn't quit playing, or they would have lost the game, and the championship. The best way to show Josh how much they cared for him was to keep playing and win the game. In the other story, the girls can come back to Mount Ellis and hike any time they want to.

A Boy and His Best Friend answers

1. (any two)
Travis calls his parents Ma and Pa
Ma drives a wagon, not a car
Travis attends a one-room school house
2. She means he has to do them every day and not get behind on them.
3. c
4. showering him with soft, wet kisses
5. Chance was Travis's shadow
6. b

Zeus vs. Typhon answers

1. the phrase *fate was with me that day* means that Zeus won the drawing to become ruler of the gods
2. b
3. dis guise
4. c
5. a
6.(any three) hurling thunderbolts, flying through the sky on winged horses, flames shooting out of the mouth of Typhon, 200 knives in Typhon's mouth, instant reattachment of toes and fingers, picking up a mountain and throwing it on Typhon, etc.
7. she is the goddess of wisdom
8. Tartarus

9. momentarily
10. a

Jack's First Christmas in Africa answers

1. He had to get used to eating strange food, and living in a hut
2. a maze ment
3. she meant she didn't really believe him when he said he was fine
4. He said *"fine, I guess"*, which doesn't sound like he means it, and he sighed
5. c

The Big 6th Grade Election answers

1. tallied
2. c
3. throw in the towel
4. to give up; to quit
5. answers will vary

Reading: Informational Texts

Gabby Douglas: Star of the Olympics answers

1. The Olympics
2. c
3. Opinion. That the Olympics take place every four years is a fact, but whether or not it's the most prestigious sports event is a matter of personal opinion. Millions of people would agree that the Olympics competition is the most prestigious sporting event in the world, but it is still an opinion, not a fact.
4. contagious
5. a family who allows someone from out of town to stay with them for an extended period of time
6. endorsement deals
7. ten
8. maneuver
9. c
10. d

Gabby Douglas: My Story answers

1. She would probably say no, because it was seeing her big sister doing gymnastics that led her to start training at such a young age.
2. Liang Chow
3. (answers will vary; here are some possible answers)
Gymnastics training is very hard
Training several hours a day is not only hard, but very boring
She missed her real family and old friends
She was injured or sick
She didn't think she was good enough to become a champion
4. This one. The other article is more focused on the Olympics and Gabby's previous accomplishments in gymnastics, but this article gives us more insight into what kind of person she is and the background she came from.
5. a

The Wonderful World of World Records answers

1. athletics
2. new records are set every year, so the book needs to updated with the new information
3. b
4. answers will vary
5. a

All About New Zealand answers

1. Lake Taupo
2. c
3. No. It is in the Southern Hemisphere, near the South Pole. America is a very long distance from New Zealand, in the Northern Hemisphere.
4. Hawaii
5. b

Earthquakes and Volcanoes in New Zealand answers

1. Answers will vary
2. 2006
3. February 3, 1931
4. 20 km
5. The previous article was written to encourage people to visit New Zealand. People tend to be scared of earthquakes, so if they knew that New Zealand has a lot of little earthquakes they might decide not to visit.

Metamorphosis answers

1. one
2. No
3. b
4. the leaves they're born on ("leaves" is also acceptable)
5. no

6. pupa
7 chrys a lis
8. Monarch
9. b
10. fas ci nat ing
11. cocoon
12. No; the baby may get around differently, but it has not changed into something completely different looking.

How to Make Spaghetti answers

1. not necessary; not required
2. following a good recipe
3. a
4. a bowl with holes in it for draining liquids from foods
5. it does not say how many servings the recipe provides

Weather Can Be Dangerous answers

1. c
2. take part | take part | engage
3. b
4. A blizzard features extreme cold and strong winds, in addition to snow.
5. c

Roger Staubach: Football Legend answers

1. d
2. c
3. con sec u tive
4. Most Valuable Player
5. to fulfill his obligation to serve in the Navy
6. the Heisman Trophy
7. d
8. answers will vary

No Ordinary House Cats! answers

1. intriguing
2. exotic
3. cheetahs; the article says they can outrun any animal over short distances
4. the jaguar; the article says no other animal can compete with its power
5. No
6. in trigu ing
7. re tract a ble
8. dies because it can't breath
9. the context is talking about the cheetah getting food by grabbing an animal around its throat
10. to inform--the article has elements of both entertainment and information, but its main purpose is to inform

Language

It's All Relative answers

1. Whoever
2. where
3. whom
4. when
5. who or that
6. which
7. Whichever
8. how
9. whose
10. that
11. where
12. which
13. which
14. how
15. that

Progressive Tense Exercises answers

1. I am watching TV.
2. I am riding my bike.
3. I am washing my hair.
4. I am eating lunch.
5. I am playing chess
6. We were sleeping when the thunderstorm started.
7. We were studying for the test because we didn't want to fail.
8. We were swimming in the deep end of the pool when the lifeguard announced the pool was closing.
9. We were reading quietly when the teacher announced a surprise quiz.
10. I was watching videos on my phone when the battery died.
11. will be playing
12. am going to be studying

13. will be watching
14. will be traveling
15. are going to be arriving

Modal Verbs Exercise answers

1. can
2. might
3. may
4. should
5. would
6. must
7. must
8. Can
9. cannot (or can't)
10. could
11. must
12. must
13. could
14. ought to
15. will

Adjective Order Exercise answers

1. d
2. a
3. b
4. c
5. d
6. c
7. c
8. a
9. b
10. a

Preposition Exercise answers

1. in
2. to
3. by
4. in
5. regarding
6. of
7. under
8. around
9. on
10. down

Find the Prepositional Phrase answers

1. before you leap -ADV
2. into things - ADV
3. across the nation - ADJ
4. in time - ADJ
5. of prevention - ADJ
6. after lunch - ADV
7. during the test period - ADV
8. between two opinions - ADV
9. except for Lawanda -- ADJ
10. off the couch - ADV

Complete Sentence Exercise answers

1. Stop right there
2. gave her grandmother a hug
3. enjoyed reading that book
4. are coming over tonight
5. think that's incorrect
6. ran a 10k
7. is 14 years old

8. revolves around the sun
9. is awesome
10. is taller than Jim

Fragment or Complete Sentence Exercise answers

1. F
2. C
3. F
4. F
5. C
6. C
7. F
8. F
9. C
10. C

Run-on Sentence Exercise answers

1. R
2. R
3. C
4. C
5. C
6. R
7. C
8. R
9. C
10. R

Homophone Exercise answers

1. principal
2. flour
3. four

4. too
5. whole
6. waste
7. it's
8. its
9. to
10. there
11. right
12. weight
13. steel
14. they're
15. two
16. stare
17. piece
18. bear
19. brake
20. son
21. hour
22. their
23. pour
24. plain
25. pair

Capitalization Exercise answers

1. NO CHANGE
2. That's Easy for You to Say!
3. Cheaper by the Dozen
4. Chicago, Illinois
5. I would like to make an appointment with Doctor Jones
6. "Be careful, Frank!" yelled Coach Johnson.
7. After the game, a reporter interviewed the coach.
8. Last year on vacation, we went to Yellowstone National Park.
9. NO CHANGE
10. Muslims believe in Allah and follow the teachings of the Koran.

11. Bill Gates was the founder of the company called Microsoft.
12. My great-grandfather fought in World War II.
13. Christmas and New Year's Day are always one week apart.
14. Dear Reverend Swanson,
15. In my opinion, no salad is complete without Italian dressing.

Commas and Quotation Marks Exercise answers

1. "Do you know what time it is?" the little girl asked.
2. "That's strange," thought Cindy, "the puppy was just here but now he's gone."
3. Mrs. Rojas said, "Please raise your hand if you're still working on the test."
4. Mom asked, "Who wants to help me with the dishes?"
5. Bonnie said, "I think that's the best field trip we've ever been on."

Coordinating Conjunctions Exercise answers

1. I'm a light sleeper, but my sister is a very deep sleeper.
2. I play soccer, and I am becoming a better player every year.
3. Do you want to play checkers, or do you want to play chess?
4. It was raining very hard, so I grabbed my umbrella.
5. We went to the zoo, and we went to the art museum.

Spelling Exercise answers

1. c
2. a
3. a
4. b
5. d
6. d
7. b
8. b
9. a

10. a

Being Concise Exercise answers

1. I arrive at school every day at 8 AM. | I arrive at school every weekday at 8 AM.
2. During the California Gold Rush
3. Joe was smiling because he passed the test.
4. If it starts raining, we'll go inside.
5. There are 50 states in America. | Currently, there are 50 states in America.

Connotation and Denotation Exercise answers

1. b
2. d
3. a
4. d
5. c
6. d
7. a
8. b
9. c
10. c

Using Punctuation for Effect Exercise answers

1. The three Rs--reading, 'riting, and 'rithmetic--form the foundation of education.
2. The big game--the one I've been telling you about all week--starts in exactly one hour.
3. As the crowd cheered him on, Rico bent his knees, swung for the fences--and struck out.
4. I can't believe I got a 100 on my math test--a 100!
5. That's the first 100 I've ever gotten on a math test--actually it's the first 100 I've ever gotten on any test.

6. My favorite author--the only one whose books I read again and again—is J.K. Rowling.
7. Four teams are left: Chicago, Dallas, New York, and Los Angeles.
8. There's only one person who can save us: Superman.
9. I only ask for one thing, class: that everyone does his or her best.
10. I had to make a decision: go to Ann's house after school, or go to Brenda's house.
11. They lost again today; that makes 20 games lost in a row.
12. It's half past five; Grandma and Grandpa should be here any minute.
13. It looks like rain; I'd better take an umbrella.
14. This is Tony's classroom; Tammy's classroom is down the hall.
15. We have to arrive at school early; we're going on a field trip.

Formal and Informal English Exercise answers

1. F
2. I
3. F
4. F
5. F
6. I
7. I
8. F
9. I
10. I

Vocabulary Exercise 1 answers

1. pupil
2. agriculture
3. fortunate
4. auditorium
5. population

6. assist
7. vertical
8. lecture
9. recognize
10. accomplish
11. curiosity
12. suggest
13. slender
14. mature
15. superb
16. seldom
17. pleasure
18. compassion
19. massive
20. admire

Vocabulary Exercise 2 answers

1. hesitate
2. annually
3. tremble
4. plead
5. biology
6. boundary
7. companion
8. thrifty
9. elevate
10. tarnish
11. circular
12. decrease
13. quench
14. foreign
15. furnish
16. request
17. coarse

18. environment
19. predict
20. absent

Greek and Latin Roots, Prefixes and Suffixes answers

1. earth
2. far
3. body
4. measure
5. heat
6. small
7. many
8. write
9. star
10. life
11. year
12. carry
13. bend
14. all
15. see
16. speech
17. sound
18. excessive
19. opposite
20. not

Similes and Metaphors Exercise answers

1. Trent turns into a bulldozer | Trent turns into a strong person who runs other players over
2. like a dream come true | it was something I had wanted to do for a long time
3. as white as a ghost | very, very pale

4. The Yankees are the 800 pound gorilla | the Yankees are a very powerful team others are afraid of
5. he's a vacuum cleaner | he eats so much it's as if he just vacuums food into his mouth
6. like a big blue blanket | the sky covers the whole world
7. Just like clockwork | the cat is as reliable as a clock
8. you're a magician in the kitchen | Mrs. Jones is an extremely good cook
9. like a giraffe | Sam was much taller than the others, so he stood out
10. You're an angel | you're a very nice person

Idioms Exercise answers

1. telling a person something that's not true but pretending that it is
2. someone who talks tough, but really isn't
3. raining extremely hard
4. go to bed
5. extremely expensive
6. got very angry
7. someone who spends a lot of time on the couch
8. going out of your way not to make someone angry or unhappy
9. wait; calm down
10. in trouble

Proverbs Exercise answers

1. the mice will play
2. home
3. before they hatch
4. louder than words
5. catches the worm
6. deserves another
7. and eat it, too
8. in one basket
9. are soon parted
10. the eye of the beholder

Antonym Exercise answers

1. hideous
2. inferior
3. rare
4. stingy
5. friendly
6. boring
7. seldom
8. temporary
9. loyalty
10. folly
11. slow
12. clumsy
13. shame
14. failure
15. liquid
16. organized
17. close
18. dislike
19. dull
20. weakness

Synonym Exercise answers

1. frailty
2. regal
3. prize
4. thing
5. leap
6. anxious
7. hilarious
8. depressed
9. shrub

10. ocean
11. total
12. cyclone
13. purchase
14. powerful
15. rock
16. foolish
17. squirm
18. city
19. intelligent
20. sleepy

Practice Test Answers

Practice Test #1

Answers and Explanations

1. A: is the best choice because paragraph 4 indicates that the story is set in spring. B, C, and D are not the best choices because the story is set in spring.

2. B: is the best choice because paragraph 16 explains that a dojo is a karate school. A, C, and D are not the best choices because they present incorrect definitions of the word "dojo".

3. D: is the best choice because the correct definition of "conferred" is "discussed." A, B, and C are not the best choices because they are not proper definitions of "conferred."

4. A: is the best choice because Joe invites Keith to the tournament so that Keith will understand that karate is important to Joe. B and D are not the best choices because they do not accurately represent Joe's attitude in the story. C is not the best choice because it does not represent Joe's main motivation for inviting Keith to the tournament.

5. Part A: B: is the best choice because Keith's attitude changes from thinking karate is boring to hoping to attend another tournament. A is not the best choice because Keith's attitude does change throughout the story. C and D are not the best choices because they do not accurately represent the change in Keith's attitude.

Part B: This sentence is from paragraph 6 and shows how Keith feels: "It sounds boring," Keith said. By paragraph 28 his attitude has changed and the story states, "Keith hoped he could attend another tournament with Joe very soon!"

6. B: is the best choice because a "green belt" properly completes the sequence. A, C, and D are not the best choices because they are not standard karate belt colors and cannot complete the presented sequence.

7. Part A: is the best choice because the primary purpose of the story is to show that karate is important to Joe. C is a good answer, but it is not the best choice because it does not reflect the primary purpose of the story. B and D are not the best choices because they do not represent themes or purposes from the story.

Part B: B: This sentence shows how committed Joe is to Karate and it shows that it is important enough to him to not skip his tournament.

8. D: is the best choice because karate is very important to Joe, so he is very likely to keep practicing it. A, B, and C are not the best choices because they do not accurately represent Joe's likelihood of continuing to practice karate.

9. Part A: C: is the best choice because it is a fact that Joe's father and grandfather both practice karate. A, B, and D are not the best choices because they are all statements of opinion instead of fact.

Part B: D: This sentence supports the fact that Joe's father and grandfather both practice karate.

10. B: is the best choice because karate is part of Joe's family heritage, as three generations of his family practice karate. A and D are good answers, but they are not the best choices because they do not demonstrate how Joe's family heritage involves karate. C is not the best choice because it does not express how karate honors Joe's family heritage.

11. A good summary of this story would read something like:

Joe invited Keith to come to his Karate tournament. At first Keith thought it would be boring and did not want to go, but once he was there he loved it. He liked learning about the sport and watching his friend compete. In the end he even decide he would like to go again.

12. C: In the story Joe says that he hopes he can reach a black belt so that he can teach karate one day.

13. C: is the best choice because the official name of the Alamo is San Antonio de Valero. A, B, and D are not the best choices because they list incorrect official names for the Alamo.

14. A: is the best choice because the author's purpose in writing "Remember the Alamo" is clearly to inform. B, C, and D are not the best choices because they represent inaccurate purposes for the story.

15. D: is the best choice because freedom was the main motivation for those who fought at the Alamo. A, B, and C are not the best choices because they do not portray the primary motivation for the Alamo fighters.

16. B: is the best choice because the Alamo was designed to serve many purposes in the community. A, C, and D are not the best choices because they do not reflect the real purpose behind the design of the Alamo.

17. D: is the best choice because it is a statement of opinion. A, B, and C are not the best choices because they are all statements of fact.

18. A: is the best choice because 184 Americans died defending the Alamo. B, C, and D are not the best choices because they are inaccurate answers.

19. II, III, IV: Jim Bowie, Davy Crockett, and General Santa Anna were all at the Battle of the Alamo. General Sam Houston fought General Santa Anna's army later, and Andrew Jackson was president at that time.

20. C: is the best choice because the story states that the Alamo is located in downtown San Antonio. A, B, and D are not the best choices because they name incorrect locations for the Alamo.

21. B: is the best choice because according to paragraph 6, the old bell is Eric's favorite artifact. A, C, and D are not the best choices because none of those things are Eric's favorite artifact.

22. C: is the best answer because it accurately completes the schedule for Eric's class trip. A, B, and D are not the best choices because they do not properly represent the events of the class trip.

23. A: is the best choice because the story says Eric was excited to see where the battle occurred. B, C, and D are not the best choices because they reflect inaccurate motivations for Eric's excitement.

24. B: is the best choice because the best definition for the word "artifacts" is "historical items". A, C, and D are not the best choices because they are incorrect definitions.

25. Part A: C: is the best choice because paragraph 6 describes Eric's favorite experiences at the Alamo. A, B, and D are not the best choices because those paragraphs do not describe Eric's favorite experiences.

Part B: A: This sentence comes from paragraph 6 and talks about one of Eric's favorite experiences.

26. D: is the best choice because the two stories both have a central theme of the history of the Alamo, linking them together. While A, B, and C are mentioned in both stories, they are not the best choices because they do not represent central themes in the stories.

27. C: is the best choice because the biggest difference between the two stories is that one is nonfiction and the other is fiction. While A, B, and D all represent differences between the stories, they are not the best choices because those differences are not as fundamental as the difference between nonfiction and fiction.

28. D: is the best choice: Uncle Eddie is qualified to teach guitar because he plays very well. A, B, and C are not the best choices because they do not represent Uncle Eddie's best qualification to teach guitar.

29. A: is the best choice because the tuning pegs of a guitar are used to help the strings make the right note. B, C, and D are not the best choices because they are not used to help tune the guitar.

30. A: is the best choice because "intently" means "in a focused way." B, C, and D are not the best choices because they do not represent accurate definitions of "intently."

31. B: is the best choice because it best completes the sequence of the story. A, C, and D are not the best choices because they do not complete the sequence according to the progression of the story.

32. D: is the best choice because the main theme of the story is to show that learning to play the guitar takes hard work. A, B, and C are not the best choices because they do not represent the main theme of the story.

33. C: is the best choice because this story is written in third person. A, B, and D are not the best choices because they represent incorrect points of view for this story.

34. A: is the best choice because Uncle Eddie feels playing the guitar will be hard, but Kari feels it will be easy. B, C, and D are not the best choices because they represent inaccurate perspectives for Uncle Eddie and Kari according to the story.

35. C: is the best choice because paragraph 14 says "Kari sighed" as the author's way of indicating Kari's displeasure. A, B, and D are not the best choices because they do not reference details included in paragraph 14.

36. B: is the best choice because Uncle Eddie is playing the "horrible music" Kari hears in paragraph 26. A, C, and D are not the best choices because they do not represent the correct person who is playing the "horrible music."

37. A: is the best choice because it is the only statement of fact from the story. B, C, and D are not the best choices because they are all statements of opinion instead of fact.

38 B: In paragraph 19, the word "bridge" is used to describe the piece of wood that holds the guitar strings.

39. There are several parts of the guitar mentioned in the story. Any four of the following are acceptable answers: body, neck, tuning pegs, strings, bridge, fingerboard, frets, and the sounding board.

40. B: In paragraph 25, Kari says "Maybe the guitar isn't for me," This sounds like she has given up.

Practice Test #2

Answers and Explanations

1. B: is the best choice because this story is set at Grandma's house. A, C, and D are not the best choices because they do not accurately represent the setting for the story.

2. A: is the best choice because the main theme of this story is that there are many different ways to have fun. B, C, and D are not the best choices because they are not main themes of the story.

3. C: is the best choice because paragraph 1 indicates that Becca thinks Grandma is "dull". A, B, and D are not the best choices because "dull" is the only word specifically used by the author to describe Becca's feelings about Grandma's house.

4. Part A: B: is the best choice because it most accurately represents the change in Becca's attitude between the beginning and end of the story. A, C, and D are not the best choices because they do not accurately describe the changes in Becca's attitude between the beginning and end of the story.

Part B: C: The point where Becca's attitude starts to change is when Grandma starts telling her about the fun things she did as a kid. Becca decides to do some of these things and she starts having fun.

5. II, III, V: In paragraph 11, Grandma talks about doing all three of these things as a kid.

6. A: is the best choice because the author's main purpose in writing this story is to entertain the reader. B, C, and D are not the best choices because the purpose of the story is not to inform, persuade, or influence.

7. C: is the best choice because it is the only statement of fact. A, B, and D are not the best choices because they are all statements of opinion.

8. B: is the best choice because the story says Becca and Grandma ate lunch in a blanket fort. A, C, and D are not the best choices because they do not accurately describe where Becca and Grandma ate lunch.

9. Part A: D: is the best choice because in paragraph 8 Becca asked Grandma to get a computer. A, B, and C are not the best choices because Becca did not ask Grandma to get a dog, TV, or car.

Part B: C: When Becca asks Grandma for a computer her response is, "We didn't have computers or game systems when I was young,"

10. B: is the best choice because Grandma has the most positive attitude in this story. A and C are not the best choices because Becca and her mom do not clearly demonstrate positive attitudes throughout this story. D is not the best choice because Grandma does have a positive attitude.

11. B: is the best choice because paragraph 22 is the first paragraph to show the change in Becca's attitude. A, C, and D are not the best choices because paragraphs 10, 24, and 26 are not the first paragraphs to show the change in Becca's attitude.

12. B: The five tribes mentioned are the Iroquois, Choctaw, Cherokee, Plains Indians, and Hopi.

13. B: is the best choice because the main purpose of dance in Native American culture is to communicate a message. A, C, and D are not the best choices because they do not accurately reflect the main purpose of dance in Native American culture.

14. A: is the best choice because the Iroquois corn husk dance and the Hopi Snake Ceremonial were both intended to bring good crops. B, C, and D are not the best choices because they do not represent the purpose of these dances.

15. I, II, IV: All of these statements can be proven as true and are not debatable.

16. C: is the best choice because in many Native American tribes the eagle feather represents strength. A, B, and D are not the best choices because they do not reflect the meaning of the eagle feather in many Native American tribes.

17. A: is the best choice because the author's main purpose in writing this article is to inform the reader. B, C, and D are not the best choices because the author's primary purpose in writing this article is not to entertain, to influence, or to persuade.

18. B: is the best choice because paragraph 1 indicates the narrator is of Cherokee heritage. A, C, and D are not the best choices because the narrator is not of Hopi, Iroquois, or Choctaw heritage.

19. A: is the best choice because this story is written in first person. B, C, and D are not the best choices because they do not accurately represent the point of view in which this story is written.

20. A: is the best choice because the main theme of this story is that Native American dancing tells a story. B, C, and D are not the best choices because they do not accurately represent the main theme of this story.

21. D: is the best choice because it is the only statement of opinion. A, B, and C are not the best choices because they are all statements of fact.

22. B: is the best choice because the story indicates the narrator was looking at the items for sale on the tables before the dancing began. A, C, and D are not the best choices because they do not accurately reflect what the narrator was doing before the dancing began.

23. A: "Pulsing" refers to the steady beating of the drum.

24. B: The last sentence of the story states, "It was an ancient story: the story of my people."

25. C: is the best choice because the importance of dancing in the Native American culture is a central theme in both stories. A, B, and D are not the best choices because they do not represent themes that are central to both stories.

26. A: is the best choice because both stories compare Native American dancing to language. B, C, and D are not the best choices because Native American dancing is not compared in these stories to music, cooking, or art.

27. C: The Cherokee are mentioned in the first story and they are the main focus of the second story. None of the others are mentioned in the second story.

28. B: is the best choice because the Spanish word for grandmother is "abuela". A, C, and D are not the best choices because none of these words mean grandmother.

29. B: is the best choice because this story is set in Tampico, Mexico. A, C, and D are not the best choices because they do not represent the true setting of this story.

30. C: is the best choice because it most accurately completes the chart of Marianna's vacation. A, B, and D are not the best choices because they do not accurately complete the chart of Marianna's vacation.

31. Part A: D: is the best choice because paragraphs 8 through 11 discuss Marianna's visit with her cousins. A, B, and C are not the best choices because they do not represent the correct range of paragraphs that discuss Marianna's visit with her cousins.

Part B: B: In paragraph 9, after meeting her cousins, they ask Jorge to play "futbol" or soccer. All of the other events occurred outside of paragraphs 8 through 11.

32. B: is the best choice because futbol means soccer. A, C, and D are not the best choices because they are incorrect translations of futbol.

33. A: is the best choice because the author wrote from Marianna's point of view to show her thoughts and feelings to the reader. B, C, and D are not the best choices because they do not represent the author's intentions in writing from Marianna's point of view.

34. C: is the best choice because paragraph 13 shows Marianna does not want to go home because she loves Abuela and loves Mexico. A, B, and D are not the best choices because they do not accurately reflect why Marianna does not want to leave Mexico.

35. B: is the best choice because paragraph 6 uses personification to describe the wind. A and C are not the best choices because simile and metaphor are not used to describe the wind in paragraph 6. D is not the best choice because personification is used, and personification is a literary device.

36. Part A: D: is the best choice because the relationship between Marianna and her grandmother is clearly loving. A, B, and C are not the best choices because they do not accurately describe the relationship between Marianna and her grandmother.

Part B: There are many sentences that can show that they have a loving relationship. One example is , "Although she was going home, Marianna knew her heart would always hold a special place for Abuela's world."

37. C: is the best choice because it is the only statement of opinion. A, B, and D are not the best choices because they are all statements of fact.

38. A: is the best choice because Marianna went to the open market with Abuela on the day of the party. B, C, and D are not the best choices because Marianna did not go to the beach, the ruins, or the supermarket with Abuela on the day of the party.

39. D: is the best choice because the main ingredient of chicle is sapodilla pulp. A, B, and C are not the best choices because they do not represent the main ingredient of chicle.

40. D: In paragraph 11 it says, "As the sun went down, they called it a tie and finally headed inside."

Online Resources

Due to our efforts to try to keep this book to a manageable length, we've created a link that will give you access to all of your online resources:

mometrix.com/resources719/ssncg4elarwb

It's Your Moment, Let's Celebrate It!

Share your story @mometrixtestpreparation